Keys of the Kingdom

by
Roy H. Hicks, D.D.

HARRISON HOUSE
Tulsa, Oklahoma

Unless otherwise indicated, all Scripture quotations are taken from the *King James Version* of the Bible.

7th Printing
Over 29,500 in Print

Keys of the Kingdom
ISBN 0-89274-330-1
Copyright © 1984 by Roy H. Hicks
P.O. Box 4113
San Marcos, California 92069

Published by Harrison House, Inc.
P. O. Box 35035
Tulsa, Oklahoma 74153

Contents

Introduction

There are many keys in God's Kingdom. Volumes would be required to describe all these keys.

In this book I deal with only a few. Space would not permit me to talk about important keys such as intercessory prayer, faithfulness, perseverance, and good stewardship, to mention only a few. Effective witnessing and Bible study would also need to be covered.

I have endeavored to limit myself to the subject of the authority Jesus gave to the Church, the power of the Church to pray the prayer of faith and to heal the sick.

I do not recall ever seeing anything in print that calls attention to the difference in praying to the Father in Jesus' Name and the use of the Name of Jesus (only) to do the works He did while on earth.

If I accomplish nothing more by writing this book than to help us return to the recognition of the power of Jesus' Name, I will feel highly rewarded. If I can stir the Church of Jesus Christ to return to the examples of the disciples in the book of Acts, then another book published will not have been in vain.

Dear reader, may you realize what it means to be a believer with the keys of the earthly kingdom of our Lord in your possession. May you be able to put a stop to Satan's activities in your life and become what our Lord intended you to become!

In order to be believers whose lives show these effects, we must first understand what great peace and victory God wills for us to have. F. F. Bosworth, in his book *Divine Life of the Body*, says, "It is impossible to boldly claim by faith a blessing which we are not sure God offers because the power of God can only be claimed where the will of God is known."

1
Calvinism And Arminianism In Balance

Webster's New Collegiate Dictionary defines *Calvinism* as "the doctrines of the French theologian John Calvin (1509-64), including election or predestination, limited atonement, total depravity, irresistibility of grace, and the perseverance of the saints. Calvin especially emphasizes the sovereignty of God in the bestowal of grace."

The opposing view was that of James Arminius (1560-1609), a Dutch Protestant who argued against the tenets of strict Calvinism, laying much more stress on the free will of man.

That same dictionary describes *sovereign* as "**1.** Chief or highest; supreme. **2.** Supreme in power; superior in position to all others;... **3.** Independent of, and unlimited by, any other...."

Like you, the author of this book stands in awe before the sovereign God of the universe.

The comparison between Calvinism and Arminianism in this book in no way is intended to take anything away from the diety of Almighty God. The question addressed is not the sovereignty of God, but rather whether or not God, in His sovereignty, surrendered part of that sovereignty in order for mankind to be free to exercise a choice of whom he would serve.

Either man is a totally depraved robot (as Calvinism would seem to imply), or else he is just born a sinner and has the ability to exercise a choice to be born again (as Arminianism would hold). It has been said that in Calvinism God is the problem...and in Arminianism man is the problem. With Calvinism, man does not have the liberty to look for the answer. With the other view he is constantly seeking to understand the "whys" of life.

The question of whether or not the Calvinist can pray the prayer of faith will always be debated. It was said of Martin Luther that he hated the book of James. This Bible book is the one which speaks of the sick calling for the church to pray the prayer of faith. (James 5:14,15.)

There seem to be so many conflicts as I read about Calvinism. At one time Martin Luther, a Calvinist, called upon God to spare his dear friend, and his friend gave credit to that prayer for saving him. Did Luther, in a time of emergency, forget his theology? Or did his friend respond in faith to Luther's outburst of anguish? Most modern-day Calvinists seem to have wandered far away from the position held by what is called a true or hyper-Calvinist.

Some Baptists pride themselves on being Calvinists, (though they may not believe in predestination), holding that since they are elected they cannot now apostasize and be lost...but on the other hand, they belie Calvinist doctrine by believing that "whosoever will may come." I have yet to meet a person (though there may be a few) of the Calvinist persuasion who has been involved in the exercising of the gifts of the Spirit and in ministry to the sick by the laying on of hands, as most of the pentecostals are.

As soon as one believes he has been delegated power and authority by God, he is at that point moving away from the teachings of Calvinism. While I do not believe that Calvinism can be balanced and remain true to the Calvinist doctrine, I do believe that Arminianism can be guided back to its true course and become more balanced.

The great danger of man's being free to choose, not only whom he will serve but how he will serve, has great risks. The imbalance that the Arminians fall into is legalism. They begin to try, in themselves, to be holy by the laying down of many rigid rules. They become, in outward show, that which they would like to be inwardly. They forget that God looks on the heart of man and not on that which he puts on or takes off.

Another imbalance of the Arminians is, while stressing the power and liberty of man's will to choose, they make salvation too contingent on man's will, placing too much value on his works and not enough on his faith. James, whose writings identify him with the Arminians, endeavored to keep this in balance as he discussed faith and works in chapter 2 of his epistle. He summarizes by saying, ''Faith without works is dead,'' proving that if a man has faith then his works or actions will prove it. (James 2:17,18.)

Some modern-day Pentecostals and holiness people are reluctant to identify with the Arminian persuasion because of the extremes that have been practiced in some groups. The problem is that when one tries to leave the Arminian side, he drifts toward the Calvinist side. In an effort not to place so much emphasis on works, if one is not careful, he soon begins to discount works totally. Even though these people are not yet saying that a person cannot be lost after receiving Jesus, they say he can only lose his salvation by great effort.

The Bible does make our position in Christ Jesus a very secure one. As we remain in Him, we are totally secure. Yet the same Word of God also warns us that we can, by our own will, go back to the mire of sin even as a dog returning to its vomit. (2 Pet. 2:22.) The balance between works and faith will always be a precarious one. It is not achieved or maintained by forsaking either works or faith, and certainly not by believing eternal security.

The balance in the Arminian view that God has delegated His earthly authority, through Jesus, to the Church by giving us the keys to the Kingdom of heaven, is also one that is difficult to maintain. Excellent Bible translators do not totally agree as to the true meaning of the Greek tenses in Matthew 16:19 upon which this position is based. Many read it to say, "What is bound, forbidden, stopped, prohibited on earth is bound, forbidden, stopped, prohibited in heaven." One translator suggests that the verse should be read, "What is bound on earth is *held in heaven* to be bound." Another one states that it should read "must already be bound in heaven."

The real key to this balance of authority is found in the finished work of the cross. Jesus, our Lord, defeated Satan, sickness, and disease. He settled the question once and for all. He took authority over this world and delegated it to us. Yet that authority must be exercised within the bounds of God's sovereignty and man's free will. We cannot bind, or take authority over, another man's will. If a human being wants to sin and begins to give himself to it, we cannot bind Satan for him.

Dr. Kenneth Hagin tells about an experience he had while praying. Satan got in between Jesus and Brother Hagin and was causing such a disturbance that Brother Hagin could not hear what Jesus was saying. He waited, expecting Jesus to do something about it. After a while, when it was evident that He wasn't going to, Brother Hagin took authority over the devil, who left. Jesus then spoke to Brother Hagin and said, ''If you had not done that, I could not have.'' Then He went on to explain to him that He could not bind Satan because He had given that power and authority to the believer. When He went to the cross, He gave all power and authority over the devil to the Church.

Paul, in Acts 27, said to the men on the doomed ship, that God, by His angel, had promised safety for all. When some of the sailors tried to escape in the lifeboats, Paul warned the centurion in charge that if these men did not stay on the ship, the ship's company could not be saved. (vv. 30,31.)

Simply put, the two illustrations above teach us that ''God cannot...unless we do.''

Jesus could only heal a few in His home town because of the unbelief. (Mark 6:5.) The key to this question of balance of authority is that we have scriptural guidelines laid down for us, and by adhering to them we can use this authority and bring glory to God by the results.

Let us not waver in our conviction that God is sovereign in His Kingdom and that He allowed Satan, by the fall of man, to be sovereign in his. But let us also never forget that Jesus has bought back that authority and delegated it to us. We, through the power of the Blood, can now rule over Satan by the authority given to us by Jesus.

Let us use the keys in balance. This is not a book on prayer, but we must remember that God can do through us only what we can accomplish through prayer and a godly life. I have found more of a godly fear and respect among the people who desire to constantly work on improving their relationship with God and with men than I have with those who view God's sovereignty as unchangeable, something over which they have no control.

2
The Healing Covenant
In the Old Testament

A covenant is a contract or agreement. The dictionary defines it as "a binding and solemn agreement made by two or more individuals." The Biblical meaning of a covenant would be the promises made by God to man. A legal contract, oral or written, is always enforceable by law and only broken at great cost to the party breaking it. Hebrews 8:6 says of Jesus, "But now hath he obtained a more excellent ministry, by how much also he is the mediator of a better covenant, which was established upon better promises."

The Greek meaning could allow us to read, "He is mediator of a *superior* contract, based on *superior* promises." The Greek word *diatheke*, translated here as "covenant," implies the making of it by one party, with penalty if the other party breaks it. It is almost as if God is saying to us, "I will never break My covenant. If you break it, you will suffer; but I will never break My part."

If we, as human beings, could ever really believe and receive this great truth, we would be invincible: **God does not fail.** He cannot. Heaven and earth would pass away before He could, or would, break His Word to us.

Let us search His Word concerning a physical healing pact made with His people, just one of the many contracts made by Him.

Did God truly make such a contract? If He ever did make an agreement to be Israel's healer, i.e., a healer of their sicknesses and diseases, did He ever break it? If He made such a physical healing covenant, did He make it only with Israel in the Old Testament, or did that healing covenant pass on to us? Was it ever acted upon by the two parties involved? Is it for us today, or was it just meant for them?

Let us go back to God's first physical healing covenant with Israel. Exodus 15:26 states: "If thou wilt diligently hearken to the voice of the Lord thy God, and wilt do that which is right in his sight, and wilt give ear to his commandments, and keep all his statutes, I will put none of these diseases upon thee, which I have brought upon the Egyptians: for I am the Lord that healeth thee."

God's covenant with His people is that not only will He not put diseases on them, but will be *Jehovah-rapha* to them. That is, He will always be the Lord God who heals them. He is not the one who makes them sick, as so many theologians teach us today.

Further confirming this healing agreement is Exodus 23:25 which reads: "And ye shall serve (worship) the Lord your God, and he shall bless thy bread, and thy water; and I will take sickness away from the midst of thee." (See also Deut. 7:15.)

Notice that God's promises are based on something we humans do—hearkening to His voice and keeping His commandments. In Exodus He says that all a person needs to do to receive His blessing is to worship (Heb. *abad*—'serve') Him. You see, when one worships His Lord and God, he must be obeying and doing God's will or it cannot be true worship. If we do that, God will bless the bread and water we consume. He promises to take away (Heb. *suwr*—'be without') sickness from us.

What a wonderful promise to us. Serve Him, worship Him, and He covenants to do His part, that is, to keep sickness away from us. Did God do this for His people Israel? Yes, for hundreds of years they lived and walked under this perfect agreement.

Psalm 105:37 says, "He brought them (the children of Israel) forth also with silver and gold: and there was not one feeble person among their tribes." The Hebrew word translated here as "feeble" is *kashal* meaning "to *totter*, or *waver*...to *falter*, *stumble*, faint or fall:...be decayed, (cause to) fail,...be weak" (*Strong's Exhaustive Concordance*).

In Deuteronomy 29:5 God says, "And I have led you forty years in the wilderness: your clothes are not waxen old upon you, and thy shoe is not waxen old upon thy foot."

What a covenant! What a God! What blessed people! Not only did God provide their daily sustenance such as food, water and shelter; not only did sickness not come upon them; but even their shoes and clothing did not wear out. This simply means that when God's presence goes with us, accompanies us, stays with us, even that which is physical, or material, reacts and functions extraordinarily because the Eternal One is there.

How important it is to practice His precious presence. Smith Wigglesworth, a mighty evangelist of another era, probably emulated this lifestyle more than anyone I have ever read about. He declared he would not go over 30 minutes without stopping to read His Bible or pray.

Do you practice God's presence? Read His Word faithfully? Engage Him in conversation? Speak often with tongues? Repeat His Word to yourself and others around you? These things provide for a consciousness of His presence for, you see, He is with us whether we acknowledge Him or not.

Did God have only one healing covenant with Israel for just forty years? Did it stop after they were settled in Canaan? If not, what happened to it?

First of all, there is no record that God ever rescinded this covenant. On the contrary, David referred to its being in operation in his day, which was many years after the Jews were well established in their homeland.

In Psalm 103:1-4 he states:

Bless the Lord, O my soul: and all that is within me, bless his holy name.

Bless the Lord, O my soul, and forget not all his benefits:

Who forgiveth all thine iniquities; who healeth all thy diseases;

Who redeemeth thy life from destruction; who crowneth thee with lovingkindness and tender mercies.

Secondly, we know that King Asa died because "he sought not to the Lord, but to the physicians."

(2 Chron. 16:12,13.) The implication here is that if he had sought God first, he would have lived out his normal life. This is not a passage of Scripture for God's people to use as an excuse not to seek medical help when they need it. But certainly in time of physical need we should seek God first.

It is well to know that King Solomon made many pacts with ungodly kings around him. It is a well-known fact that to confirm these treaties, Solomon married many pagan princesses—seven hundred of them, in fact. It is also well known that when these brides came from their heathen lands, they also brought with them a large entourage of servants.

Included in this group of people were their personal physicians (today we could call them witch doctors), who used incantations and mysterious potions in their healing art. It is very possible that it was one of these physicians whom Asa sought.

God made a healing covenant with Israel—and He never violated or terminated it. If it failed to be effective, it was because of Israel's violation of the terms. (Be sure to read carefully the 28th chapter of Deuteronomy.)

3
The Healing Covenant
In the New Testament

Did God, as so many pastors have contended, discontinue His healing covenant in the New Testament? Did He favor Israel only? Did He have compassion for the Old Testament people only and not for those who would be saved by the death of His Son Jesus? Did His compassion for His people end?

What about a comparison of covenants? Did they, in the Old Testament, have a better covenant than we can expect in the New Testament? Was He *Jehovah-rapha*, "the healing one," only for Israel, or is He going to continue to be the healing one for the Gentiles as well? Do we, as Gentiles, have a covenant as good as the one God made with the Jews?

> **But now hath he (Jesus) obtained a more excellent ministry, by how much also he is the mediator of a better covenant, which was established upon better promises.**
>
> **Hebrews 8:6**

Yes, by all means, our covenant is not only as good as anything made with Israel, it is better and superior in every way.

Some denominational theologians have sold us a "bill of goods." Even to hint that divine healing stopped with the Old Covenant has done great disservice to our covenant-making, compassionate God.

We must, after establishing the Old Testament covenant, examine Scriptures to see if our Lord Jesus extended the healing covenant to the Gentiles, or did it end, as suggested by the aforementioned clerics?

> **When the even was come, they brought unto him (Jesus) many that were possessed with devils: and he cast out the spirits with his word, and healed all that were sick:**
>
> **That it might be fulfilled which was spoken by Esaias the prophet, saying, Himself took our infirmities, and bare our sicknesses.**
>
> **Matthew 8:16,17**

Most all opponents of the physical healing covenant will freely admit that Jesus, the mighty, powerful Son of God, did heal the sick. He did work outstanding miracles. He did turn the water into wine. He did walk on the water. He did calm the storm. But, they say, He did this only to prove that He was the Son of God.

What nonsense! Jesus healed out of great compassion. His love flowed out to the sick and the demon oppressed. Jesus simply portrayed the outpouring of God's nature and compassion.

Can we find any scriptural proof that our Lord Jesus passed this healing power on to His followers? If so, can we prove that Jesus did not intend for this power to end with the disciples? Did He ever indicate that His twelve disciples would be the only ones who would work miracles, or did He pass such miraculous power on to *all* who would believe in Him?

In Mark 16:15-18 we read these words spoken by Jesus to His disciples just before His ascension into Heaven:

> Go ye into all the world, and preach the gospel to every creature.
>
> He that believeth and is baptized shall be saved; but he that believeth not shall be damned.
>
> And these signs shall follow them that believe; In my name shall they cast out devils; they shall speak with new tongues;
>
> They shall take up serpents; and if they drink any deadly thing, it shall not hurt them; they shall lay hands on the sick, and they shall recover.

Yes. Jesus did say that those who believe in Him would cast out devils and lay hands on the sick with great results.

But what about the controversy among some scholars as to whether or not this passage was in the original Biblical texts? My answer to this question is that the Bible is so written that a person can end up believing whatever he wants to believe. I will admit that there is disagreement over this passage. But even if a person wanted to believe that these verses were false, or not part of the Scriptures, he would still have to believe that the disciples heard Jesus say this because they went out and did it!

If we do not believe the veracity of Mark 16:17,18, then we cannot believe the whole book of Acts! The disciples did go forth in His Name and worked the works that Jesus worked. They got this power and authority from somebody, and we believe they got it directly from our Lord Jesus and the Great Commission recorded in Mark's Gospel!

Both Irenaeus and Polycarp, pupils of John the Apostle, quote from the Great Commission in Mark 16. *Bodily Healing and the Atonement* by Dr. T. J. McCrossan, carries quotations from many of the great early Church fathers on this subject, all verifying these great truths as belonging to the Church. (See page 41 of this notable book.)

There are some who might reluctantly admit that some of the earlier believers did work miracles. They might even admit that the early Church fathers of a hundred years after the disciples noted the continuation of miracles up to their day. But these same people would say that miracles are not for today because, "...when that which is perfect is come, then that which is in part shall be done away" (1 Cor. 13:10). Yes, this is a verse of Scripture from the Bible. No, it has nothing whatsoever to do with any covenant God ever made anytime, anywhere.

Such thinking presumes that when the Word of God was printed and the final book was added to the other 65 books, then God's healing covenant made with Israel and the Gentiles could be considered to be void because "that which is perfect is come," meaning the Bible is completed.

James 5:14-16 states:

> **Is any sick among you? let him call for the elders of the church; and let them pray over him, anointing him with oil in the name of the Lord:**
>
> **And the prayer of faith shall save the sick, and the Lord shall raise him up; and if he have committed sins, they shall be forgiven him.**
>
> **Confess your faults one to another, and pray one for another, that ye may be healed. The effectual fervent prayer of a righteous man availeth much.**

Powerful advice. Powerful command. For it is a command, not an option. When a person is sick, he is commanded to turn to the Lord, whom James teaches, is still healing. But wait a minute! There are some who say that James was only writing to the Jewish Church because he was Jewish. If that were true, then Paul, who was Jewish, also wrote only to the Jews and not to the Gentiles. In fact, with that kind of reasoning, the Gentile Church could not say that it had a Bible, because all of the writers were Jewish.

In his short book of five chapters, James refers to "my beloved brethren" three times, meaning that he is writing to New Testament saints. As Dr. T. J. McCrossan, the eminent Greek scholar puts it, "Whenever you find the expression 'beloved' (*agapetai*) or 'my beloved brethren' (*adelphau mou agapetai*) these expressions always, without one exception, refer to the church saints."

Note that James said to call for the elders of the church (*ekklesia*) and not the elders of the synagogue. James also makes it clear he is writing to saints living in the last days, and I assume that includes you and me. The main purpose of this chapter is to establish that there is a commandment for all New Testament believers to observe when they are sick.

Note the responsibilities of those who are sick:

1. Call for the elders to come.
2. Have them anoint with oil in the Name of the Lord.
3. Pray the prayer of faith.

Note the responsibilities of the church:

1. To have godly elders (leaders in the church) ready to respond to the call of the sick in their church.
2. To carry oil with them for that purpose.
3. To pray the prayer of faith.

Note the responsibility of the Lord:

1. To hear that prayer.
2. To raise up the sick one.
3. To forgive his sins.

Yes! That better covenant, based upon better promises, does most certainly extend the physical healing covenant to the Gentile Church. If all of the healing miracles taking place in this present day could be recorded in a book, you would be unable to lift it!

One of our foreign missionaries returned home sick and was told by several doctors that she was filled with cancer and that there was no hope of recovery. All tests, including x-rays, confirmed their diagnosis. After a time of fasting and prayer and anointing with oil, the prayer of faith was prayed in Jesus' Name.

Our missionary said, "I believe I am healed, but it will take surgery to prove it." She proceeded with the scheduled surgery. The doctors found the cancer, removed it and found that the roots were dried up. Many of the surgeons came by her bed, for they had seen the x-rays, and remarked, "You have indeed experienced a great miracle!"

Despite so many of these miracles, the Church will continue to point out the few who have received prayer, and yet died. The author will be one of the first to point out that this does happen. I do not have the answer to that any more than I have the answer to why good Christians, even pastors, sometimes return to their old sinful ways. I do not stop preaching salvation because of these failures; neither will I stop preaching the healing covenant because of failures! I would trust that we all will continue to preach the whole counsel of God's Word as it is and not go by the results we see with our physical eyes.

4
The Neglected Bible Verse

Do I mean to imply by this title that there is a verse in the Bible that the Church ignores? Is there such a thing as a verse being overlooked? If so, is it intentional, or is it a verse that has remained hidden?

There is such a verse and a very important one, regardless of whether it has simply been overlooked or been ignored.

Let us together take a good look and you will have to make up your own mind about it. We have already quoted James 5:14,15 in the chapter on the healing covenant in the New Testament. These verses are well known by pentecostals and practiced by them, but somewhat ignored by the evangelicals.

The next one, verse 16, is not preached, or practiced, by pentecostals (or anyone else) as far as I know. WHY? Perhaps it is because we are afraid of it, because of pride—a feeling of, ''I don't want anyone to know about my faults.'' That line of reasoning has to be a little humorous, because all of us know we have faults.

I, as an author of a book that deals with this subject, feel that we have overlooked the importance of this verse. We have ignored its relationship to our failure to be healed according to the preceding 14th and 15th verses which teach us to anoint with oil and pray for the sick.

James 5:16 says, "Confess your faults one to another, and pray one for another, that ye may be healed. The effectual fervent prayer of a righteous man availeth much."

I believe the important thing that we overlook is that this verse is placed here to suggest there can be a reason why we are not healed by the Lord, even after the prayer of faith has been prayed.

There can be something amiss, something wrong, and we know it cannot be the Lord and His faithfulness to heal.

Please notice also that the problem cannot be the sin of the person being prayed for, either, because that sin is taken care of in verse 15: "...if he have committed sins, they shall be forgiven him." The problem is that we as a Church have not been faithful and obedient in confessing our FAULTS.

No, I do not mean that we are to set up booths in our churches to hear people confess their *sins*! Articular confession to a priest is not implied here. Thank God, the sin question is taken care of by our Lord Jesus Christ and the shedding of His blood for the atonement. What the Bible is talking about here are the "faults" that go unconfessed, faults that may not keep us out of heaven, but which can keep us from being healed in our physical bodies.

Faults are usually the result of our soulish nature and, in many cases, are very commonplace. Such faults are so commonplace that we all seem to have them. They are so ordinary that we all seem either to be content to live with them, or to go along placing no importance on them. But God does not ignore them.

He cannot ignore them. That is why this verse is here and why so many Christians are sick, and remain sick even after they are prayed for by the church or elders.

Let me give you an illustration. In one of our churches where I was ministering, a young man came up to me bringing his seven-year-old son. This is the story he related to me.

"My son was born with a double hernia. The doctors were amazed because it was a rarity to be born that way. They informed me that it would be wiser to operate on him before he began to crawl and become physically active.

"After much prayer, we gave our parental consent and the surgeons went in and put the two hernias back in place, and we thought it was all over and taken care of by that surgery.

"The doctors were all very shocked when the hernias burst out again. They assured us that they had never heard of that happening before, especially since the child was not yet physically active.

"We really prayed hard, sought God, and even took our pastor to the hospital to anoint our son and pray for him, but to no avail. It seemed that there was nothing left to do but to go back for surgery.

"The surgery again seemed to be successful, and we thought the trial of our faith was over and that our little boy would be all right. But to the amazement of all, especially the doctors, the hernias ruptured again.

"This time, I really sought God with all my heart, baring my soul before Him. It was brought before me by the Holy Spirit that my father and I had had a trying time ever since I was old enough to remember. I thought I had forgiven him after I became born again and that all was well.

"As I sought God and prayed, He revealed to me that I had not really, truly forgiven my father. I want you to know that I went to him and took care of it, and things were made right between us. When the doctors examined my son, they were amazed. *The two hernias had gone back in of their own accord!*"

This true story is just one of several I have heard. Many of God's people have been prayed for, even anointed, and have sought God for healing. Sometimes the whole church prays, and nothing happens. The healing does not come until after careful searchings of heart and seeking after God to reveal hidden resentment, unforgiveness, etc. Then, when God reveals these hidden faults—and the person is quick to seek forgiveness or repent of his faults—he is gloriously healed!

I know of a lady who had sought God for seven years for her husband to be saved. Finally she went to her pastor to find out, if possible, why her husband was not saved. The Lord revealed unforgiveness she had held in her heart since her teenage years, something that she had forcibly put out of her mind. She took care of it, asking our Father to forgive her of her bitterness and to help her to forgive others. The next day, which was a Sunday, when the altar call was given, the lady's husband gave his heart to the Lord. For years her unforgiveness had hindered her prayers.

I could go on with scores of illustrations of such victories being won after faults were confessed, repented of, and forgiven. God our Father loves us very much. He sent Jesus His Son to die for us and to pay the price, not only for our eternal salvation, but also for the physical needs of this life.

Because some translations read, "Confess your *sins* (rather than *faults*) one to another," there has been some confusion. The Greek word in this verse is *paraptoma*. *Strong's Exhaustive Concordance* defines it as, "a side-slip...i.e. (unintentional) *error* or (wilful) *transgression*:—fall, fault, offence, sin, trespass." W. E. Vine renders *paraptoma* as "trespass," "a blunder," "to fall away." (Vol. IV, p. 154.)

One of the difficulties, as already noted in another chapter, is due to the translators' having access to different manuscripts. Some of these, those considered to be the most reliable, have inserted the same Greek word *hamartia* which is used in James 5:15. Those "sins" (*hamartia*) are forgiven when the Lord saves and raises up the sick one who has been anointed and prayed over by the elders.

In James 5:16 the *King James Version* of the Bible uses the word "faults" because it is translated from manuscripts called *Textus Receptus*. This word "faults" certainly makes sense with regard to the context. In the 15th verse the Lord takes care of the *sin* (*hamartia*) problem. In the 16th verse He takes care of the *faults*. They are forgiven when the person confesses them. A safe prayer, in any situation, would be, "Father, if I have anything against anyone which I am not aware of, please reveal it to me."

Dear reader, if you have been anointed and prayed for by the elders (leaders in the church) and you are still not healed, then by all means go to your heavenly Father in prayer and ask Him to reveal anything to you in the way of faults, unforgiveness, resentment, pride, selfishness, a highly independent spirit, or any other thing you may have overlooked that needs to be confessed and forgiven. He will hear you and forgive you and then, and only then, will the effectual fervent prayer, either by you or the elders, avail.

5

The Key to
the Prayer of Faith

James 5:14,15 teaches us that as we anoint with oil in the Name of the Lord and pray the prayer of faith, it will save the sick and the Lord will raise him up and restore him completely, even to the forgiving of his sins. Complete restoration!

The great question we Christians must ask ourselves is, "Do we know how to effectively minister to the sick person? To the one who calls for help from the leaders of the church?" According to the Scriptures we are the ones who are to come to the aid of the sick. Judging by the small number of healing testimonies we hear, compared to the great number of people who are anointed, we will have to admit that we really do not know how to pray that prayer. What is *the prayer of faith*?

First of all, the prayer of faith is a prayer that is prayed in faith. Therefore, by definition, it cannot be a prayer that is prayed without faith.

In this passage from James, the word translated "prayer" is the Greek word *euche* which means "prayer" or "a vow." This word adds a powerful dimension to the prayer of faith when we think of prayer in the sense of taking a vow. When we pray, it is like entering into a contract with God. "I vow (in my prayer) to God Who (in turn) vows to heal." When one can stand over a sick person, anoint him with oil and say, "I vow, or take a vow of such confidence in God, that you will be raised up and restored completely—body, soul, and spirit," something has to happen!

It is easy to see that such confidence must have a firm foundation. So firm a foundation that it would cause one to stop by a lame man who has not walked in forty years and say, "Silver and gold have I none; but such as I have give I thee: In the name of Jesus Christ of Nazareth, rise up and walk" (Acts 3:6).

Do you remember what Peter did then, after saying these words? He reached down and took that lame man by the hand and pulled him up. The man, as you know, was gloriously healed! Peter would have looked rather silly or ridiculous if he had acted in presumption by reaching down to lift up the man while saying to himself in his heart, "What if it doesn't work?"

No, Peter had the confidence of a person who could *vow* that something was going to happen. And, of course, it did, and that for all to see. Reading the account of it in the book of Acts still blesses us today.

Did the apostles know something we have never learned? How is it that they never prayed long prayers for the sick as we do today? Faced with that same situation, we today would gather around that sick, helpless man and have a prayer meeting! Peter did not pray to God, that *He would reach down and heal that poor lame man*. Peter is the one who *reached down and pulled him up!* He did the act. Yes, I said *he* did it—and he did it in the Name of Jesus! He did not pray lengthily, as we do today and have been doing for over 2,000 years. We, the Church, continually pray and petition God to act and to do it all for us. What did the disciples know that we seem to have missed or forgotten? What is it that they understood that we need to understand today?

Peter did not pray over the lame man at the gate. Neither did the Apostle Paul pray over or petition God for the lame man in the city of Lystra. (Acts 14:8-10.) He did not call for a prayer meeting of the saints. Paul simply said with a loud voice, "Stand upright on thy feet" (v.10), and the man leaped to his feet and walked, just as the cripple whom Peter healed in Jesus' Name.

Peter, when he was called to the death bed of Dorcas (Acts 9:36-43), did not gather all the ladies around and bombard heaven for the resurrection of the dead saint, as we might do today. Instead he put them all out of the room. One reason he dismissed them was because they loved Dorcas so much and were so overcome with emotion that they could have been a hindrance to him, rather than a help. Peter did pray. The Bible doesn't record what he said. It is *not* recorded that he asked God to raise Dorcas from the dead. Peter then turned to the dead woman and commanded her to rise. As a result, she was raised from the dead and there was great rejoicing!

Peter follows this pattern of active faith throughout the book of Acts, and it teaches us so very much concerning ministry to the sick and raising of the dead.

Let me repeat the question: "Did they, the disciples who sat under the ministry of our Lord Jesus, understand something about ministering to the sick that we have not understood?'' Since it seems to be true that they healed in the book of Acts, not by *requesting* action from the Father in prayer, but by *taking* action themselves, then it should at least cause us to go back to the teaching of our Lord Jesus on this subject and examine it more carefully.

Let us go to the Gospel of John, to one of the times when Jesus was teaching His disciples on the subject of prayer. This passage deals directly with the question: ''Do we ask God our Father to heal and work miracles, or do we work them ourselves in Jesus' Name as the apostles did in the book of Acts?''

In chapters 14 through 17 of the book of John, Jesus gives a long discourse on prayer. In chapter 14, verse 10, He challenges the disciples to believe that He is in the Father and the Father is in Him. This was in answer to Phillip who had requested Jesus to show them the Father and that would be sufficient.

In verse 11 Jesus exhorts them to believe in Him because of the works He is doing. They should not need anything other than the works in order to believe He came from God. That should be sufficient.

In verse 12 Jesus goes on to challenge them by saying that, if they believed on Him, they would do the very same works He was doing, and even greater works. That would be all of the proof they would need to convince the world that He and the Father were one.

But how would they do these important works that would cause all men to believe and see the Father? Jesus makes it so very plain. In verses 13 and 14 He tells them: ''And whatsoever ye shall ask in *my* name, that will *I* do, that the Father may be glorified in the Son. If ye shall ask any thing in *my* name, *I* will do it."

What a powerful statement is John 14:12. Yes, it is there. Jesus said that we who believe on Him could (and would) do the very same works He did. What were the works that Jesus did? They are listed in the Bible: heal the sick, the lame, the blind, the deaf and the dumb, the lepers; deliver the ones bound by evil spirits and the demon possessed; raise the dead; etc.

Why is it that we do not see the book of Acts duplicated today? Is it because we do not comprehend the teaching of the Scriptures? Is it because we do not act upon that teaching as the disciples did after they had sat under the ministry of our Lord Jesus?

They must have fully understood what He meant for they went forth remembering His words and doing the works that He did. We have those same words. We have those same instructions. Our problem is that it seems too simple. We have complicated it by our theology of the Trinity.

For nearly two thousand years we have prayed and asked God our Father to work the miracles that *we* should have been working. Jesus taught His disciples that *they* would do the works He did and *they* would do them in His Name.

You might say, "How can you be so dogmatic? How can you say that the disciples were taught to work miracles in Jesus' Name?" Simply because that is what they did. They went out and worked miracles in His Name!

In John 14:12-14 Jesus instructs them to ask in His Name and He, Jesus, not the Father, would give them what they asked so that the Father would be glorified in the Son. We have, by our traditional teaching, turned that around. Now we ask the Father to work the miracle in Jesus' Name—so now it seems that Jesus is glorified, not the Father.

The intention of Jesus in this teaching is to answer the disciples' questions about the Father. To them it seemed that if Jesus was really Who He claimed to be, then He should reveal the Father to them. Jesus would not do this. He asks them to believe in Him because of the works He is doing.

Jesus proceeds to command them to continue to do His works so that the Father can be glorified in the Son. Then in verses 15 through 21 He goes on to talk about His returning to His Father so that the Holy Spirit can come into the world. The continuation of the work of Jesus on earth to glorify the Father is now left in the hands and lives of the disciples and all of the converts and followers who would be baptized and called believers.

The overlooked key to the prayer of faith, or to the working of any miracle, is the fact that it must be done in the Name of Jesus. Jesus strongly taught His disciples to ask *Him*, not the Father, and they literally practiced what He taught them. He said to them, ''Anything you ask in My Name I will do.'' (John 14:14.) He did not teach here, concerning the works and miracles He did, to ask the Father in His Name. The teaching as to what we are to ask the Father to do in Jesus' Name comes much later in His discourse.

We Christians are so bound by traditions of how we have always understood the Bible, that when it is suggested that we are to use Jesus' Name, and not ask the Father to work the works that Jesus did, people get angry. "The very idea!" they say. But Jesus, not this author, is the One Who said it.

The disciples must have thoroughly understood exactly what Jesus taught, because they went forth and worked miracles in that Name above all names, the wonderful Name of Jesus!

They did understand that they were to pray to God the Father in the Name of Jesus. Jesus is the One Who taught them to pray, "Our Father which art in heaven..." (Matt. 6:9). They also prayed to God in the book of Acts. In Ephesians 3:14 the Apostle Paul enjoins us to pray to the Father when he says, "For this cause I bow my knees unto the Father of our Lord Jesus Christ."

Jesus' disciples understood the difference between praying to God the Father in Jesus' Name and the working of miracles in Jesus' Name. The difficulty is that we modern-day disciples have never tried to understand that difference. We should try. As far as I know, no recognized Bible commentary has ever noted the difference. Perhaps the Holy Spirit is stirring us to work great miracles in these last days.

Clear delineation of what we are to do in Jesus' Name, and what we are to ask the Father to do, is distinctly drawn in the Scriptures. (Read the following chapter on the key of prayer to the Father to see what is promised by praying to God in Jesus' Name.)

To conclude this chapter, I urge you to remember that the key to all miracles of healing is the fact that we are to do the same works that Jesus did, as so clearly stated in John 14:14-16. The key to the prayer of faith, to miracles, is to use that strong and wonderful Name of Jesus.

6

The Key of Prayer
to The Father

And in that day ye shall ask me nothing. Verily, verily, I say unto you, Whatsoever ye shall ask the Father in my name, he will give it you.

Hitherto have ye asked nothing in my name: ask, and ye shall receive, that your joy may be full.

These things have I spoken unto you in proverbs: but the time cometh, when I shall no more speak unto you in proverbs, but I shall shew you plainly of the Father.

At that day ye shall ask in my name: and I say not unto you, that I will pray the Father for you:

For the Father himself loveth you, because ye have loved me, and have believed that I came out from God.

I came forth from the Father, and am come into the world: again, I leave the world, and go to the Father.

His disciples said unto him, Lo, now speakest thou plainly, and speakest no proverb.

Now are we sure that thou knowest all things, and needest not that any man should ask thee: by this we believe that thou camest forth from God.

Jesus answered them, Do ye now believe?

John 16:23-31

There are two methods of prayer taught in the Gospels. One is a prayer to the Father in Jesus' Name.

The other is a prayer directly to Jesus. If we fail to differentiate between the two, then we seem to have a great contradiction in the Bible.

Some might suggest that it really does not matter to whom the prayer is addressed, or in whose name we pray, because God sees the heart. They would say that perhaps we are just dealing in what might be termed technicalities. As a matter of fact, the author has presented the question of prayer in open forum situations, and 99% of the answers were as the above—that it really does not matter how we pray. My response to that was, "Then are you saying that we could pray in the name of Mohammed or Buddha?" Christians are always quick to respond negatively to that implication, quickly affirming that it *does* matter how we pray.

During the discourse in the latter chapters of John's Gospel, Jesus talks to His disciples about many things. Usually He taught the public in parables, but with His disciples He spoke much more plainly. Now He gets to the heart of His relationship with His Father. The Jews were so indoctrinated in the principle that "the Lord our God is one Lord" they were having difficulty in receiving the teachings of Jesus, particularly His assertion that He and the Father were One.

Not only does Jesus present Himself as part of the Godhead, He now introduces the Comforter, who is the Holy Spirit and third Person of the Trinity! This is the One Jesus said He would ask the Father to send to be with the believers after He had gone back to the Father.

In John 14:11-14 Jesus speaks to His disciples about accepting His relationship with God based on the works that testified of Him, or simply believing Him for His works' sake.

In John 16:23 He surprises them with the statement, "In that day you will ask Me nothing." This follows hard after His statement in the same discourse that, "Anything you ask in My Name, that will I do." (John 14:14.) Is there a contradiction here?

Jesus is saying to His disciples here, "The day is coming when you will no longer ask Me any more questions." All Greek scholars agree that the verb has that primary meaning. You must remember that they, the disciples, were constantly asking Him questions. One commentator suggested that they even asked stupid and foolish questions because there was so much to learn. We would doubtless have done the same.

Now, Jesus is telling them that henceforth they will be requesting things from the Father in His Name, and He, the Father, will give them what they request.

Jesus is changing from talking about miracles and works the disciples will *do*, to things they will be *receiving* from the Father by going to Him in Jesus' own Name. He says, "Hitherto (up until now) you have not gone to the Father in My Name." (v. 24.) Jesus is very bold to even insinuate to a Jew that he can no longer pray directly to God the Father! This is the way the Jews had been taught to pray for generations!

Jesus borders on blasphemy, but He continues His discourse because He is confident that the disciples love Him and believe in His works and miracles.

"Ask," He says, i.e., "Ask (the Father in My Name), and you shall receive, that your joy may be full" (v. 24).

Ah! Here is great insight. Now we can begin to see the difference between what we are to ask the Father in Jesus' Name and what we are to ask (command) in Jesus' Name for Him (Jesus) to do.

The miracles referred to in John 14:12 (where the Father was to be glorified in the Son) differ vastly from those things we would receive from the Father for our own personal joy. The latter are things such as would be received by a child from his father.

Miracles, the works of Jesus, are not supposed to cause joy in the one working the miracle. Jesus stopped the disciples from rejoicing over the miracles they did when He sent them forth with power. He told them not to rejoice over the sick being healed and demons cast out, but rather to rejoice over the fact that their names were written in heaven. (Luke 10:19,20.)

The Church, especially the pentecostals, have not always obeyed this injunction. It seems that we are constantly looking for a miracle to rejoice over. It is not reasonable to expect that a person receiving a miracle will not be happy, but his *greater joy* is to be in the knowledge that his name is written in heaven. This great truth is to take precedence over all rejoicing, for salvation is the greatest miracle one can ever receive and we are to constantly rejoice because we are sons of God.

In John 15:7,8 Jesus told His disciples that by going and asking the Father in His Name they would receive. In the same passage Jesus talks about fruit bearing. Now we know at least two things for which we are to approach the Father in Jesus' Name: That which makes a contribution to our personal happiness, and that which will cause us to become fruit bearers (soul winners).

Even though most people rightly believe that the Lord's Prayer is a prayer that contains principles more than form, yet it still fits in very well with the concept that teaches us that we can go to the Father for our own well-being, that we can make requests to the Father concerning ourselves and our loved ones. Praying for our daily bread, extending forgiveness, being delivered from evil, will certainly make great contributions to our happiness. Our Father truly desires this for His children.

Romans 8:32 says, "He that spared not his own Son, but delivered him up for us all, how shall he not with him also freely give us all things?" In Matthew 18:19, Jesus taught that if any two could agree together on earth concerning anything they asked of God in prayer, it would be done for them by His Father in heaven.

There is nothing in these scriptures to discount going to the Father in prayer requesting a miracle for one's own self and his personal joy. But when a believer is to work a miracle on someone else (doing the works Jesus did), this is to be done *in Jesus' Name, by Jesus through us.* His promise is that He is with us, working as He did in Bible days! (Matt. 28:20; Mark 16:20.)

Jesus continues, in His discourse in John 16, to break down the traditional barriers in the minds of the

Jews which prevented them from accepting and understanding the concept of the Trinity. Notice verses 25-27:

> **These things have I spoken unto you in proverbs: but the time cometh, when I shall no more speak unto you in proverbs, but I shall shew you plainly of the Father.**

> **At that day ye shall ask in my name: and I say not unto you, that I will pray the Father for you:**

> **For the Father himself loveth you, because ye have loved me, and have believed that I came out from God.**

Now Jesus continues to reveal the nature of His Father by teaching the disciples how much the Father loves them. He informs them that when they go to the Father in His Name that He, Jesus, will not have to prevail upon or persuade the Father to do what they ask.

The evangelical theologians have not presented an accurate picture of Jesus as our High Priest. In the Old Testament the High Priest did not go into the Holy of Holies to intercede for Israel with words. His high priestly ministry was totally accomplished by taking into the Holy of Holies, where dwelt God's presence, the blood of an animal as sin offering and holding it up before the Lord.

Contrary to popular religious teaching, Jesus, our High Priest and Intercessor, is not turning to the Father and pleading on our behalf, showing the Father His wounded side and hands and begging God, "For My sake, please do what they ask." Jesus fulfilled the New Testament contract by taking in His own blood once and for all. That was all that was necessary for Him to do. His intercessory work is accomplished by His presence at the right hand of God. Our preaching that Jesus has to turn to a reluctant God and talk Him into doing something is not scriptural!

We do not have a reluctant Father, one who only responds to pressure from His Son; but rather ours is a loving, kind, and very generous heavenly Father Who delights in answering our prayers. Jesus teaches that God will give us whatever we ask because He loves us, and because we love His Son and believe that He came forth from the Father.

In verses 29 and 30 notice how the disciples now fully understand everything Jesus has taught them and will no longer be asking questions:

> His disciples said unto him, Lo, now speakest thou plainly, and speakest no proverb.
>
> Now are we sure that thou knowest all things, and needest not that any man should ask thee: by this we believe that thou camest forth from God.

With this statement they show that they understand what Jesus said to them in verse 23, "You will not need to ask Me questions anymore."

Whether or not you and I can totally understand what is written in this chapter is beside the point. Often I see a shocked look on the faces of believers when there is even a question raised as to which things we are to ask the Father, and which we are to ask (demand) in Jesus' Name.

The point is that it seems perfectly clear that the disciples understood. They *did* pray to the Father God. They spent much time in prayer, as we should. The writings of the church fathers bear this out. But in the book of Acts, the disciples did not ask God to heal the sick or to cast out the evil spirits for them. They, themselves, healed the sick and cast out evil spirits in Jesus' Name! Let us do the same and go forth in the power of that Name.

7

The Keys in Context

Whom do men say that I the Son of man am?

And they said, Some say that thou art John the Baptist: some, Elias; and others, Jeremias, or one of the prophets.

He saith unto them, But whom say ye that I am?

And Simon Peter answered and said, Thou art the Christ, the Son of the living God.

And Jesus answered and said unto him, Blessed art thou, Simon Barjona: for flesh and blood hath not revealed it unto thee, but my Father which is in heaven.

And I say unto thee, That thou art Peter, and upon this rock I will build my church; and the gates of hell shall not prevail against it.

And I will give unto thee the keys of the kingdom of heaven: and whatsoever thou shalt bind on earth shall be bound in heaven: and whatsoever thou shalt loose on earth shall be loosed in heaven.

Matthew 16:13-19

Moreover if thy brother shall trespass against thee, go and tell him his fault between thee and him alone: if he shall hear thee, thou hast gained thy brother.

But if he will not hear thee, then take with thee one or two more, that in the mouth of two or three witnesses every word may be established.

And if he shall neglect to hear them, tell it unto the church: but if he neglect to hear the church, let him be unto thee as an heathen man and a publican.

> Verily I say unto you, Whatsoever ye shall bind on earth shall be bound in heaven: and whatsoever ye shall loose on earth shall be loosed in heaven.
>
> Again I say unto you, That if two of you shall agree on earth as touching any thing that they shall ask, it shall be done for them of my Father which is in heaven.
>
> For where two or three are gathered together in my name, there am I in the midst of them.
>
> Then came Peter to him, and said, Lord, how oft shall my brother sin against me, and I forgive him? till seven times?
>
> Jesus saith unto him, I say not unto thee, Until seven times: but, Until seventy times seven.
>
> Matthew 18:15-22

It has been observed that the Bible is so written that one can find confirmation of anything which he has already made up his mind to believe! The deeper into humanist teaching a man delves, the more likely he is to try to make Bible interpretation fit a systematic mold of human logic.

The reason the Jewish scholars missed out on the advent of Jesus' birth, and their heaven-sent Messiah, was that they tried, as many do today, to make the interpretation of all scriptural passages fit into what is called "contextual interpretation."

The following is evidence of such errors in interpretation. After the death, burial, resurrection and ascension of Jesus, the writers of our New Testament quoted certain verses chosen from the Old Testament, applying them to Jesus—verses such as: "For these things were done, that the scripture should be fulfilled, A bone of him shall not be broken" (John 19:36 referring to Ps. 34:20). "After this, Jesus knowing that all things were now accomplished, that the scripture might be fulfilled, saith, I thirst" (John 19:28 referring to Ps. 69:21). "And about the ninth hour Jesus cried with a loud voice, saying, ...My God, my God, why hast thou forsaken me?" (Matt. 27:46 from Ps. 22:1). "They said therefore among themselves, Let us not rend it (Jesus' robe), but cast lots for it, whose it shall be: that the scripture might be fulfilled, which saith, They parted my raiment among them, and for my vesture they did cast lots" (John 19:24 referring to Ps. 22:18).

The champions of contextual interpretation say that these verses could not refer to Jesus because to do so they would have to be taken out of context. We believe the writers of the New Testament were divinely inspired when they quoted texts from the Old Testament, and we receive such texts as such.

In the same way, some of our most highly trained Bible expositors have missed the mark. These men (who have studied theology books all of which thus far have been written by ardent Calvinists or by those who lean toward Calvinism) have come up with what I believe to be errors of interpretation. At least 90% of all Christians, up to this present day, are products of this Calvinist school of thought. Thus, our Bible colleges are filled with their writings.

Their belief, that we cannot accept the teaching of Jesus that He gave the keys of the kingdom of heaven to His Church, is based primarily on a misinterpretation of the passages of Scripture found in Matthew 18, not Matthew 16.

Let us look carefully at Matthew 16 first. Dear reader, be very careful. Many people have missed this great truth and, as a result, have become prey to the spiritual and physical destruction that Satan seeks to bring upon every believer.

In Matthew 16:18 Jesus is talking about building His Church. He has just told Peter, "...thou art Peter (Gr. *Petros* a [piece of] *rock*), and upon this rock (Gr. *petra*, a [mass of] *rock*) I will build my church." To my knowledge, not one Greek scholar has ever said that Jesus meant to build His Church upon Peter. We will let that subject rest with antiquity.

That Jesus was talking about His Church is accepted by all. That He gave His keys to the Church has, in latter times, become controversial.

The disagreement is not that Jesus did, or did not, give the keys to the disciples. He did. But scholars do not agree that He also gave them *to us* to claim for *this day in which we live.* They believe that the keys were not given to us for use in this day—except to settle disagreements in the Church. This view is held today by probably 80 to 90% of all evangelicals. They teach that miracles were only performed by the disciples and ended at their demise.

The questions is, was Jesus talking only to His disciples or, dear reader, was He talking to His Church? Did He give the keys to the kingdom of heaven to only a few in that day, or did He surrender them completely to His Church so that now He works on earth only through His born-again Church?

Could He have spoken these words in jest? Does He yet retain all authority to select only a few to whom

He gives faith and authority? Did He really mean it when He said, after His resurrection, "These signs shall follow them that believe; In my name shall they cast out devils; they shall speak with new tongues; they shall take up serpents; and if they drink any deadly thing, it shall not hurt them; they shall lay hands on the sick, and they shall recover" (Mark 16:17,18)?

Do we work only as He appoints, or does He go with us to confirm His Word? Let us assume that Jesus was being straightforward with us—that He did give us the keys and will bind what the Church binds, will loose what the Church looses. Immediately a chorus of voices will arise and say, "The Bible clearly defines the use of the keys. In Matthew 18 Jesus is talking only about forgiveness and quarrels among church members."

Let us go to Matthew 18:15 and examine the context to see if the Calvinists are correct in saying we do have some use of the keys, but they are only to be used when there is a family disagreement. In verses 15 and 16, Jesus is continuing His discourse which began in verse 11 relative to God's concern for the lost. It is not the will of the Father that even one should perish. This is always the Father's priority.

In verses 16 and 17 Jesus takes care of the faults and schisms that arise within the Church. This does not pertain to those outside of it. He is teaching here and elsewhere that we are to handle these difficulties within the Church and not seek outside legal help. If one, feeling he has been offended, refuses the power assigned to the Church, then the Church has the power and authority to put him out. He then would be regarded the same as a heathen. What mighty authority.

Jesus is still talking about His concern for souls, both outside and inside the Church. Now He goes back and picks up (from the former discourse) the power of the Church and He speaks of the authority He said He would give by granting the keys of the kingdom of heaven to the believers.

To summarize this thought, let us go over it again. In His discourses of Matthew 16 and 18, Jesus is talking about lost souls, those who are outside the Church. Then He proceeds to talk to his disciples about the authority of the Church, *within* the Church, to settle quarrels and disputes. One would miss the powerful impact of this teaching if he thought that the keys of the kingdom were given to the Church simply to settle mere quarrels or misunderstandings.

Most all scholars agree that when the Bible uses the phrase "kingdom of God" it is referring to God's heavenly Kingdom and when it says "kingdom of heaven" it is referring to the earthly Kingdom. Some believe that the terms are used interchangeably. "Kingdom of heaven" is first used in Matthew 3:2 where John the Baptist says, "Repent ye: for the kingdom of heaven is at hand." Adam Clarke, the noted Bible commentator, says that the Kingdom of heaven is frequently used by the rabbinical writers and always means the purity of the divine worship and the blessedness which a righteous man feels when employed in it. To illustrate: If Jesus means the earthly Kingdom when He says to the Church, "Whatsoever ye shall bind on earth shall be bound in heaven," then He means we are to use the keys here on earth, and He will back that use in heaven. It also proves by the use of the word "earth" that Jesus refers to the earthly Kingdom.

The word "whatsoever" makes it very clear that Jesus means more than just settling quarrels in the Church. "Whatsoever" will be better defined by our Lord Jesus when He tells us in John 14:12 that we who believe will do the works that He did. When He uses the word "whatsoever," it applies to the use of the keys and can be interpreted to mean works such as healing, power over Satan, etc. Its connotation and application is certainly more far reaching than the mere settling of Church quarrels.

If Jesus did not truly give the keys of the kingdom to us, then we have no authority on earth, and the use of His Name to resist Satan is not warranted because heaven cannot back us. Remember, if Jesus had not referred back to Matthew 16 we would have to say that Jesus meant only that we had authority to settle quarrels.

Not only did Jesus give us the keys, but we can understand and receive this truth, both contextually and out of context. Remember, the reason we know the disciples heard Him correctly is because they went out and used the keys! We have the entire book of Acts as stirring proof that they used the keys for far more than just settling arguments.

One of the main reasons why I teach the power and authority of the Church to use the keys is because of their effectiveness in stopping accidents and all works of the destroyer.

The Calvinists readily ascribe to God the blame for all accidents and catastrophes. They have done such a thorough job in their preaching and writing that the insurance companies picked up on it and have put a clause in their policies negating all responsiblity if they can prove the mishap was ''an act of God.'' I could easily imagine that many insurance writers have heard a great number of these heavy sovereign sermons in their churches.

I know that God does not need me to defend Him, but please allow me to lift my voice in strong protest. My Bible teaches me that God, my heavenly Father, is a good God. (Nahum 1:7; Romans 2:4,11; 11:22.) God does not delight in seeing His children mangled and bruised any more than you or I, as parents, would allow our own dear children to be involved in a severe accident so they might learn an important lesson.

Margaret, my dear wife, and I have analyzed every accident or near-accident we have ever encountered personally. In every case God has been faithful to give a prior warning. Sometimes we refer to this warning as a premonition. It could come in a dream, or by a heavy feeling, sometimes through a fellow believer. Or the person may be warned in his own spirit to change his plans, to stay home, or even to delay a trip.

Someone once said to a young boy, ''I'll see you in church on Sunday.'' The boy answered, ''Yes, if you don't see my name in the obituary column first.'' This statement causes me to believe that he had some portent of impending misfortune. Indeed, he was killed in an accident the next day.

In another case, a pastor and his wife were awakened in the night, feeling that one of their church members was in imminent danger. They immediately went to prayer and the man was warned. The next day when he went to work, his foreman told him to climb up and release a cable on an oil derrick.

The man answered and said that he could not, because he had been warned by God that if he did he would fall and end up at the feet of the foreman, beheaded. Another worker, who laughed and scoffed at his words, climbed up the derrick. He released the cable, it whipped around and severed his head and he fell to the ground.

There are many, many illustrations such as these, but suffice it to say, our people, even in most pentecostal churches, are not taught what to do when they have premonitions or warnings. One of the reasons is that the Calvinist teaching has so affected our way of thinking that many people seem to have developed a fatalistic attitude of "what is to be, will be."

No, dear saint. Be sensitive. If you receive a warning, use the keys. Put a stop to the accident. If you do, God will stop it in heaven.

The help you need is not automatic. You must learn to use the keys at your disposal.

8

Abraham, Father of Faith

O foolish Galatians, who hath bewitched you, that ye should not obey the truth, before whose eyes Jesus Christ hath been evidently set forth, crucified among you?

This only would I learn of you, Received ye the Spirit by the works of the law, or by the hearing of faith?

Are ye so foolish? having begun in the Spirit, are ye now made perfect by the flesh?

Have ye suffered so many things in vain? if it be yet in vain.

He therefore that ministereth to you the Spirit, and worketh miracles among you, doeth he it by the works of the law, or by the hearing of faith?

Even as Abraham believed God, and it was accounted to him for righteousness.

Know ye therefore that they which are of faith, the same are the children of Abraham.

Galatians 3:1-7

I do not believe that any book on the subject of divine healing and the prayer of faith for the sick would be complete without a chapter on Abraham, the Father of Faith, Friend of God. Not only is he Israel's father, but also our father of faith.

His example is the beginning of the faith walk, that which sets in concrete the faith principles we are to use in the New Testament church age. Even though the writers of our Bible mention Abel, Enoch, and Noah, as well as many others when speaking of faith and obedience, it is obvious that much of their attention was called to Abraham and Sarah.

Especially do we notice that, by faith, Abraham left his home and nation at God's command, not knowing where God would lead him. Let me emphasize again that he obeyed God's Word and command totally by faith. He was willing to leave his own homeland, to go wherever God commanded, to live in tents and settle in an alien land—all because he believed God, took Him at His Word and trusted Him completely.

The Apostle Paul, in writing to the Galatians in chapter 3 called them "foolish" (KJV). Some translations use the word, "stupid." *The Amplified Bible* calls them "poor and silly and thoughtless and unreflecting and senseless" because they were not continuing on in faith, but were relying on the flesh and the law.

Paul continues his discourse by reminding his readers that they did not get their start in this new experience in Christ Jesus, their Messiah, by obeying the law (works) but by hearing and believing the message of faith in Christ. He chides them (and any reader still bound by legalism), saying they are guilty of being senseless, silly, thoughtless, unreflecting, and foolish. If we, too, think we can depart from faith and go back to dependence upon the flesh, then these adjectives describe us also.

The writer of Galatians goes on to talk about Abraham, and all he received from God. He especially emphasizes that he was declared righteous (i.e., pronounced totally free from the condemnation of guilt and sin, and made perfect in right standing with Almighty God Himself) by believing God.

Just think of it, a walk of faith—relying on and trusting in and adhering to the Word of God—makes one perfect in His sight! That person's past is forgiven and forgotten!

So many people today go by how they feel, or whether or not their prayers are answered, or how things are going—either good or bad. Thus feelings become their thermometer for their relationship and right standing with God. Because of this misconception, their confidence in God's hearing and answering their prayers is based on a wrong premise.

Notice Galatians 3:9: ''So then, those who are people of faith are blessed and made happy and favored by God [as partners in fellowship] with the believing and trusting Abraham'' (AMP). Notice that the emphasis is on trusting and believing, i.e., taking God at His Word as Abraham did.

Being blessed with Abraham means not only being an heir with him, but receiving all the benefits that go with the blessings of God, including health and prosperity (well-being).

In Paul's letter to the Romans, he again refers to Abraham. He demonstrates in a very positive way that Abraham's righteousness is a result of his faith. (Please read the 21st chapter of Genesis. It will bless you.)

Abraham, greatly blessed as he was, was not immune to trials and tests. Some zealous faith teachers miss this point in their endeavors to emphasize the blessings of the faith life. Abraham's faith and trust were tested to the breaking point, even as were Job's. But in the end both men were gloriously delivered. It was as though the trials faded in the light of the blessing received, even as a mother soon forgets the pain of childbirth because of the joy of her newborn child.

We now come to a portion of Scripture that is both controversial and misunderstood. I am referring to the passage in Romans 4:17-21 which deals with Abraham's age. Here we read that when all hope was gone, Abraham refused to allow his great age and the deadness of Sarah's womb to hinder faith. He trusted tenaciously that they would some day have and raise their own son who would be born of their own union, and not of surrogate parentage.

Inasmuch as the author already has written a book on this subject, he will not take the space to talk about it here. Rather, the focus of our attention will be directed to certain aspects of the original manuscripts which seem to contradict each other. The question under consideration is: Did the Holy Spirit of God want us to know that Abraham *did*, or did *not* consider his own body, his age, Sarah's body and her age? Can one pray the prayer of faith either for himself or for another without considering the odds against him? Is there a contradiction in translations?

The following is from the *King James Version* of Romans 4:19,20:

> And being not weak in faith, he considered not his own body now dead, when he was about an hundred years old, neither yet the deadness of Sarah's womb:
>
> He staggered not at the promise of God through unbelief; but was strong in faith, giving glory to God.

Note the words, "he considered *not* his own body."

Now, let's notice how this passage reads in *The American Standard Version*:

> And without being weakened in faith he considered his own body now as good as dead (he being about a hundred years old) and the deadness of Sarah's womb.

Note that this version states that he *did* consider his own body. The contradiction is not among the translators, but the manuscripts from which the translations were made.

The *King James Bible* was translated from the manuscripts called *Textus Receptus*. Almost all other translations are made from what is commonly called "the original manuscripts." Actually, all are copies. There is no such thing today as the "original letters," the original manuscripts having long since been lost. Why, then, the difference in the existing manuscripts?

Many believe that the copies of the original, from whence most of the newer translations were made, were tampered with to make them read what the copiers thought they should be saying. Some believe that early-day clerics weakened the account of the virgin birth and deity of our Lord. I have a tendency to accept that theory.

I believe the *Textus Receptus* is correct in stating that Abraham considered *not* his own body. The word *consider* means "to give careful regard to something, to keep it before one's eye, and in one's mind intensively, at all times." This we know Abraham could not have done and still have had faith—nor can we.

I believe that Paul in his original letter would have said, "Abraham did not keep before him constantly his age and Sarah's dead womb." Twentieth century translations seem to bring out the balance between the two extremes.

Though Abraham was nearly a hundred years old, yet his faith did not fail him, even when he thought of his own body, then utterly worn out, and even though he remembered that Sarah was past the age of child bearing. We can see that he acknowledged the fact of the situation, but that it was only a passing thought in his mind.

Yet we cannot allow ourselves to read into any translation any suggestion that Abraham was not aware of how old he was. He knew. He also had to know, by observation, how old Sarah was and that her womb was dead. However, even with this full understanding, he *did not* consider these facts (that is, dwell on and keep them before him constantly). Let us learn a lesson on exercising the Abraham kind of faith!

Suppose, for example, you are sick. You do know your physical condition. You are well aware of the pain, of what the doctor has said about your physical state. It would be ridiculous for you to go around saying you did not know you were ill. Abraham did know his situation, but he did not dwell on it. It was not part of his conversation. His conversation was about what God said about it.

What do you do when someone asks you, point blank, how you feel? Do not lie, and say you feel well. Just say, "I serve a God who has made a healing covenant with me. He is the One Who is constantly healing me. I have been anointed and prayed for. I will be all right." Say it in faith. The prayer of faith works through the Abraham kind of faith!

Many people confuse facts with truth. What a doctor says to you may be facts as he sees them. But you have truth. The truth of God's Word. The fact about Lazarus was that he was dead; had been dead four days, in fact. The truth, only Jesus knew—He could and would raise Lazarus from the dead. The facts did not interfere with Jesus' exercising truth. Facts do not interfere with truth today either.

Abraham knew the facts but he also knew a great truth. He served a God who calls things that are not as though they were. (Rom. 4:17.) Notice that God can call things that "be not" as though "they were." We, being His children, can do as our Father does. One of the great weaknesses in "faith confession" is that people sometimes try to call things "that be" as though they "were not." It is important to make a careful distinction between calling into existence something which is not and denying the existence of something which is!

Let me illustrate. When you are sick and feeling terrible, if someone asks you how you feel and you answer, "Never felt better!" you are lying! That statement is simply not true. You are calling things "that be" as though they "were not," and that is a delusion. In this case you must claim things that "be not," i.e., healing for your body, as though "they were," and they will be! You can say: "As a child of God, and by faith, I will be all right because with His stripes I am healed." You are then trusting in God's Word. You are calling into being, by faith, that which you do not yet have. To say that you are well is calling that which is as though it were not.

Let us follow Father Abraham in his example. He knew all of the facts against him, but gave thanks to God and called into being that which was not.

9

The Great Key of Prayer

> And when the day of Pentecost was fully come, they were all with one accord in one place.
>
> And suddenly there came a sound from heaven as of a rushing mighty wind, and it filled all the place where they were sitting.
>
> And there appeared unto them cloven tongues like as of fire, and it sat upon each of them.
>
> And they were all filled with the Holy Ghost, and began to speak with other tongues, as the Spirit gave them utterance.
>
> **Acts 2:1-4**

There are two chapters about prayer in this book. One deals with when to pray to the Father in Jesus' Name, and the other about when to go directly to Jesus. In one portion of Scripture our Lord said, "Whatsoever ye shall ask the Father in My Name, He will give it you," and in another place he said, "Anything you ask in My Name I will do."

In this chapter I want to deal with another great available source of help, one that is seldom utilized by the Christian Church. I am referring to the kind of praying that involves the third person of the Trinity, the precious Holy Spirit. It was He of whom Jesus spoke in the same discourse in chapters 14 through 17 of the Gospel of John. Jesus said He would return to the Father, and when He did, He would send another

Comforter. This Comforter, we now know, came on the day of Pentecost.

This great phenomenon is recorded in great detail in the second chapter of the book of Acts. What a notable miracle! This miracle is as great as any that our Lord Jesus worked while here on earth. Because of what took place at Pentecost the third person of the Trinity is now indwelling mortal, fallible, weak human flesh. This gift from God our Father now will enable a weak, untrained, uneducated fisherman to stand before a multitude and preach one of the greatest sermons ever recorded by the pen of man. (Acts 2:14-36.) As a result of this outpouring of the Spirit, the Church was birthed, and three thousand people were saved.

If the only great benefit that came to the Church that day was the anointing, it would be worth it to be able to speak with tongues as they did. Peter explained that this promise, the outpouring of the Spirit and the speaking with tongues, was for everyone present there and for all who would ever be called. (Acts 2:39.)

The anointing to preach and teach and bear witness is only part of the work of the Holy Spirit. He also convicts the world of sin, of righteousness, and of judgment. (John 16:8.) But there is yet another great benefit of the baptism in the Holy Spirit.

Romans 8:26,27 says, ''Likewise the Spirit also helpeth our infirmities: for we know not what we should pray for as we ought: but the Spirit itself maketh intercession for us with groanings which cannot be uttered. And he that searcheth the hearts knoweth what is the mind of the Spirit, because he maketh intercession for the saints according to the will of God.''

Please notice that this same precious Holy Spirit, given on the Day of Pentecost to bring conviction and anointing, to provide us the ability and power and authority to preach God's Word, is now presented by the Apostle Paul as a faithful companion who will help us to know how to pray.

How regrettable it is that speaking with tongues has met with such violent opposition from the majority of Christianity. Many an evangelical preacher has preached against the baptism with the Holy Spirit and speaking with tongues. As a result, very few Bible readers will examine this portion of God's Word with any degree of open-mindedness.

Please examine this great truth with me, laying aside your prejudice and all you have heard against it.

God's Word is true. God would never allow His Word to mislead us. The Holy Spirit is our helper and has come to aid us with our prayer life. He is to help us to know what to pray for as we ought.

One of the great ''infirmities'' we Christians have is our own mind. It cannot grasp the deep things of God. The Greek word translated ''infirmities'' implies that our not knowing for what to pray is a sickness or weakness.

If our finite minds are not capable of grasping or understanding the deep things of God, how then can we pray effectively? We cannot, without the third person of the Trinity helping us. The word *helper* in the Greek language simply means "one who takes hold together with us against something."

The one who prays is the initiator, not the Holy Spirit. In order to truly pray in the Spirit, the believer must begin to speak with tongues, in a language not known by him. If the pray-er only uses his own vocabulary, he is restricted to praying only about things he knows. If he does not know about the desperate needs of others, he cannot pray for them. But the Holy Spirit knows everything. As we pray in the Spirit, it is He who now makes intercession through prayer for the needs of others or for the will of God to be done on earth, with groanings which cannot be uttered.

Concerning the prayer ministry of the Holy Ghost, Montgomery's translation of Romans 8:26 reads: "...the Spirit also takes hold with us in our weakness...." *The Amplified Bible* says, "...we do not know what prayer to offer nor how to offer it worthily as we ought..." The Bible translator Joseph Rotherham renders these "groanings which cannot be uttered" as "sighings unutterable." Goodspeed calls them "inexpressible yearnings." Berkeley explains them as "sighs too deep for words." *The New English Bible* says, "...but through our inarticulate groans the Spirit himself is pleading for us...."

One thing stands out very clearly about this type of praying. It is not a known tongue and it is audible, not silent. If one were to keep silent only and hope that the Spirit was making intercession through him, his silence would not initiate any action!

In verse 27, this is further amplified by the statement that the Holy Spirit is making intercession for us "according to the will of God." Only the Spirit of God knows, truly knows, what we ought to pray for and how to do that praying. The word "intercession" suggests more than meditation or silence.

Praying with the Spirit as a great key is further taught in 1 Corinthians 14. This chapter is greatly misunderstood by many evangelicals and pentecostals alike. If one approaches this chapter thinking that there is just one use of tongues, he will miss the importance of tongues as a great prayer key.

Speaking in tongues in the Church has many uses. First Corinthians 14:1-4 says: "Follow after charity, and desire spiritual gifts, but rather that ye may prophesy. For he that speaketh in an unknown tongue speaketh not unto men, *but unto God*: for no man understandeth him; howbeit in the spirit he speaketh mysteries. But he that prophesieth speaketh unto men to edification, and exhortation, and comfort. He that speaketh in an unknown tongue edifieth himself; but he that prophesieth edifieth the church."

Verses 14 through 17 of the same chapter say: "For if I pray in an unknown tongue, my spirit prayeth, but my understanding is unfruitful. What is it then? I will pray with the spirit, and I will pray with the understanding also: I will sing with the spirit, and I will sing with the understanding also. Else when thou shalt bless with the spirit, how shall he that occupieth the room of the unlearned say Amen at thy giving of thanks, seeing he understandeth not what thou sayest? For thou verily givest thanks well, but the other is not edified."

When interpreted, speaking in tongues in church is compared equally with prophecy. (v. 5.) It is a gift to be exercised. Notice tongues are also a sign to the unbeliever. (v. 22.) This sign was certainly in evidence on the Day of Pentecost when many doubters became believers because they heard the disciples speak in many diverse tongues and languages. Some of the most dynamic verses in the Bible are those which have to do with tongues as a powerful prayer tool.

Please try to clear your mind of all you may have heard and read against praying in tongues in the Church today. Let the Word of God speak truth to you. A person who is praying with unknown tongues is not talking to men. It is not a language understood by man, but by God only, and it is to God he is speaking. No man on earth understands him. This is not a duplication of Acts 2:1-12 when men *did* understand and marveled. Praying in tongues is speaking mysteries or secrets known only to God.

Notice 1 Corinthians 14:14 where the Apostle Paul makes it very plain that praying in the Spirit is just that—prayer. It is *a prayer of the spirit* and our understanding is bypassed. I like *The Amplified Bible* version of this verse best because the amplification brings out the true Greek meaning:

> **For if I pray in an [unknown] tongue, my spirit [by the Holy Spirit within me] prays, but my mind is unproductive—bears no fruit and helps nobody.**

How greatly this verse attests to the truth found in Romans 8:26,27. How can any theologian explain away praying in tongues when it is confirmed so positively by at least these two references or witnesses?

This is the Biblical requirement for acceptance of the correctness and veracity of doctrine.

Of course, there are times when we are to use both methods of prayer—praying with the Spirit and praying with our own known language. Since the Word declares we do not know what to pray for as we ought, it should not take in-depth thinking to conclude which is the best way to pray.

The voices raised against the use of tongues today like to quote Paul when he said in verse 19, "Yet in the church I had rather speak five words with my understanding, that by my voice I might teach others also, than ten thousand words in an unknown tongue." We in the pentecostal movement agree whole-heartedly with Paul and we practice public teaching in a language understood!

There is a humorous element in the argument of those who are against tongues. They omit the 18th verse of 1 Corinthians 14. Here the Apostle Paul said, "I thank God that I speak in [strange] languages more than any of you or all of you put together" (AMP).

Would Paul be against praying in tongues if he practiced it more than all to whom he was writing? Certainly not. He must have done a lot of praying in tongues. Every great man I have known, who preaches the whole counsel of God, does a lot of speaking with tongues.

Another greatly overlooked verse in the 14th chapter of 1 Corinthians teaches a wonderful way to give thanks. This too is by speaking in tongues. The Bible, the same Bible the evangelicals claim to believe, teaches that when you give thanks in tongues you "do well." (vv. 16,17.) Again, *The Amplified Bible* brings out the true Greek text:

> **Otherwise, if you bless and render thanks with [your] spirit [thoroughly aroused by the Holy Spirit], how can anyone in the position of an outsider, or he who is not gifted with [interpreting of unknown] tongues, say the Amen to your thanksgiving, since he does not know what you are saying?**
>
> **To be sure, you may give thanks well (nobly) but the bystander is not edified—it does him no good.**

When you pray in tongues, not only are you giving thanks well, but even *nobly*.

All would agree that a public restaurant would not be the place to ask the blessing in a loud voice, using your prayer language. However, in the presence of a teachable non-pentecostal, you might dare to inform him that the Bible teaches that when you bless and give thanks with the Spirit you are doing a good thing. Then you might ask, "Would you mind if I gave thanks over this food with my prayer language?" If he gives consent, I am sure he would be edified and blessed.

We must close our comments on this great key, insamuch as space will not permit a complete exegesis. An entire book would be required to contain it.

Following is an explanation that may encourage you to use your prayer language. Please do not allow the devil to sit on your shoulder, as it were, and tell you that your prayer language doesn't sound like a language to him. Do as I do. Tell him, "I'm not talking to you!"

When you pray in tongues, you are talking to God. If some theologian dares to ask you, "How do you know you are talking to God?" just inform him, in a loving way, that the very same Bible that teaches that you can be saved by believing on Jesus, also teaches that he who speaks in an unknown tongue is talking to God.

Please do not go by feelings or by the sound of your unknown tongue. Believe the Word of God and act on it.

There are literally hundreds of illustrations and testimonies available today concerning the results of using one's prayer language, i.e., of praying in the Spirit. But if the Word of God will not convince the skeptic, then I assume hundreds of illustrations and testimonies will not convince him either!

Those of us who already believe and act on the Word of God take advantage of this blessed privilege, sometimes without any visible results. However, even when there are no visible results we notice a deepening of our spirit to understand more easily the things of God not readily understood by the natural mind. There are enough visible results to convince even the most doubtful skeptic that it does pay to use one's prayer language.

Many missionaries, home on furlough, have related mighty supernatural deliverances as a result of prayer in the Spirit. More than once some sweet saint of God has inquired of a missionary about a particular time that she had been impressed to pray in the Spirit for him, and has found it to be the very same time that the missionary was experiencing a mighty miracle.

A few years ago, at which time the author lived in Portland, Oregon, a large United Airlines jet crash-landed in the area. The plane came down in a heavily populated section of the city, among giant Douglas fir trees, and skidded across a busy intersection. There was only a 10% fatality rate. The outcome was so miraculous that the headlines in the newspaper the next day referred to it in that manner.

The author watched the TV news report of the first camera crew and reporters to arrive at the scene of the crash. The first person to be interviewed was a young man who was a Spirit-filled Christian. He told the reporter, "When the stewardess asked the passengers to prepare for a crash-landing, I turned to my family and said, 'I guess it's time to pray,' so we prayed in the Spirit." This means they used their prayer language earnestly! I have since talked with that young man, and he confirmed what we had seen and heard on the TV news report.

Many of us remember the miraculous escape from death of Jim Brady, the Presidential Press Secretary who was felled by a bullet to the brain during the assassination attempt on President Reagan. We heard the TV anchor man announce that Brady had died. Some of the doctors knew he was clinically dead. One of God's Spirit-filled believers, a Secret Service man, was on assignment in the corridor of the hospital as Jim Brady was being rolled by on a stretcher. The man told me that he felt God move him to lay his hand on Brady's body and to pray in tongues. Many of us believe that God's power was at work that day!

Many, many are the results of being obedient to the Word of God. Continue to believe in His truth and power Trust the Holy Spirit to know what to pray for, and how to pray in a language that man cannot understand. God understands and answers the prayer of the Spirit.

10
The Word—A Key

If the Calvinist view of God is correct, there is nothing you and I can do but hope we are predestined and elected. If we are among those fortunate ones thus chosen, then a sovereign God has to see to it that we are protected and provided for.

Surely if that kind of awesome power surrounds us, and if neither Satan, the arch enemy of God, nor mankind can lay a finger on us, then we do not, as James suggests, need to resist the devil. If God has chosen us, we are home free, with little or no effort on our part.

However, if we come to the conclusion that the Arminian view of God is correct, that He has delegated to man whom He created the responsibility for his own soul, then we must arm ourselves with all of the available armor and ammunition that God has provided and use the keys that are available to us.

Since neither Scripture nor logic supports the Calvinist point of view, we must do all that we can to serve our God who so loved us that He gave us His best gift, His Son.

I have established that the Scriptures clearly teach that Christ gave the keys to the Kingdom of heaven to us. It is our duty and responsibility to determine what those keys are and to make good use of them.

Let us consider something with which I believe most Christians would agree—the most important key is indeed the Word of God. Notice the importance that Moses placed upon the Word before Israel:

> And these words, which I command thee this day, shall be in thine heart:

> And thou shalt teach them diligently unto thy children, and shalt talk of them when thou sittest in thine house, and when thou walkest by the way, and when thou liest down, and when thou risest up.

> And thou shalt bind them for a sign upon thine hand, and they shall be as frontlets between thine eyes.

> And thou shalt write them upon the posts of thy house, and on thy gates.

> Deuteronomy 6:6-9

Notice the importance of the Word of God to Joshua as Israel prepares to go in to conquer the promised land:

> This book of the law shall not depart out of thy mouth; but thou shalt meditate therein day and night, that thou mayest observe to do according to all that is written therein: for then thou shalt make thy way prosperous, and then thou shalt have good success.

> Joshua 1:8

Notice also the importance of the Word in the book of Psalms:

> But his delight is in the law of the Lord; and in his law doth he meditate day and night.

> Psalm 1:2

> Thy word have I hid in mine heart, that I might not sin against thee.

> Psalm 119:11

As you read the Word in your own private devotions, always notice how much prominence and honor the saints of the Bible accorded the Word of God.

No one can deny its importance. God, through His Word to Israel, emphasized His Word as a tower of strength to them. They were to abide by it and obey it. If they would do so, then it would be a lamp unto their feet and a light to their path. (Ps. 119:105.)

Solomon notes the significance of the Word, by his words in Proverbs 4:20-23:

> **My son, attend to my words; incline thine ear unto my sayings.**
>
> **Let them not depart from thine eyes; keep them in the midst of thine heart.**
>
> **For they are life unto those that find them, and health to all their flesh.**

The wisdom contained in the book of Proverbs is received by both Calvinists and Arminians alike. Good! It should be received by all!

Solomon says that we are to attend, give full attention to, and examine the Word. Give yourself totally to the Word, be absorbed by it, incline your ears to it, because faith cometh by hearing it. Notice that this very wise man is not only talking to Israel, but to all who will receive wisdom and be highly benefited by the Word. Observe, too, that life and health are received by use of this great key.

In chapter 6, verses 20-22, Solomon goes on to emphasize the importance of this key:

> **My son, keep thy father's commandment, and forsake not the law of thy mother:**

> Bind them continually upon thine heart, and tie them about thy neck.
>
> When thou goest, it shall lead thee; when thou sleepest, it shall keep thee; and when thou awakest, it shall talk with thee.

Notice, please, as we move through the Word of God, that the prophets pick up the importance of this key. Isaiah writes in chapter 59, verse 21:

> As for me, this is my covenant with them, saith the Lord; My spirit that is upon thee, and my words which I have put in thy mouth, shall not depart out of thy mouth, nor out of the mouth of thy seed, nor out of the mouth of thy seed's seed, saith the Lord, from henceforth and for ever.

The prophet is emphasizing the importance of the Word of God as a key, not only to be kept in the heart, but also to be proclaimed by the mouth.

Let us move into the New Testament to note the great emphasis that Jesus places on the Word of God. His first recorded encounter with the devil came after He had fasted for forty days and nights. This placed our Lord in a very vulnerable position. Satan will usually come during the time when we are at our weakest. Guard those times in your life, for he is waiting to attack.

> Then was Jesus led up of the spirit into the wilderness to be tempted of the devil.
>
> And when he had fasted forty days and forty nights, he was afterward an hungred.
>
> And when the tempter came to him, he said, If thou be the Son of God, command that these stones be made bread.

But he answered and said, It is written, Man shall not live by bread alone, but by every word that proceedeth out of the mouth of God.

Matthew 4:1-4

Jesus proved the value of the key of the Word by relying on it to overcome our sworn enemy, the devil.

But he that received seed into the good ground is he that heareth the word, and understandeth it; which also beareth fruit, and bringeth forth, some an hundredfold, some sixty, some thirty.

Matthew 13:23

This key not only protects, but, if heeded, will bring forth much fruit.

If ye abide in me, and my words abide in you, ye shall ask what ye will, and It shall be done unto you.

John 15:7

This key, the Word abiding in your heart, as you abide in Christ, will cause your prayers to be answered.

Perhaps the greatest scripture to prove the Word of God as an important key in the earthly Kingdom would be Romans 10:17:

So then faith cometh by hearing, and hearing by the word of God.

Without faith we cannot please God. (Heb. 11:6.) Faith comes and remains very strong only by the Word of God. What a key! It defeats Satan, produces fruit, and brings forth and increases faith!

These Scriptures on the Word of God, so important to the Arminian theology, cannot have the same blessed significance to a follower of the Calvinist doctrine. If a person believes God has *chosen* him to go

83

to heaven, then he has no real need of the Scriptures. How could he ever lack faith? How could Satan possibly overcome him? Why would he need the admonition in Ephesians 6:17 to take the sword of the Spirit, which is the Word of God, if Satan cannot defeat him or take his salvation from him?

In my first book, *Use It or Lose It—The Word of Faith*, the Word of God is emphasized as it is used in the Greek as both *rhema* and *logos*. Go to your Greek sources and check these two words and mark them in your Bible. You will notice that usually *rhema* is that which comes out of the mouth, the spoken word. (Matt. 4:4.) *Logos* is the revelationary knowledge of God. (John 1:1.) We should read the *logos* and go our way speaking the *rhema*.

Many, many of God's people are defeated by trials and tests because they neglect this important key— the Word of God. Please, dear reader, set a discipline to follow in reading Scripture. If you do not, the enemies of Satan and the flesh will see to it that other things will interfere to keep you from the Word.

I am sure that we would be astounded if we knew how little actual time was spent in the Word of God by many Christians, sometimes even pastors. If we could determine how few could call forth, from memory, portions of the Word, we would be even more surprised.

What I am saying is, regardless of whether Christians believe in the teaching of Arminius, or that of Calvin, most of them live as if they believe they do not need to put forth much effort. They just coast along.

Notice the level of commitment spoken of as we get to the book of Revelation, the last book of the Bible:

And they overcame him by the blood of the Lamb, and by the word of their testimony; and they loved not their lives unto the death.

Revelation 12:11

The Word of God as a key can be best illustrated as we compare it (as the Bible does) with a sword. (Eph. 6:17.) A sword is a weapon that is both defensive and offensive. Which of the two do you think requires the most skill? If it is defensive, then we should memorize the verses that teach us how to deal with Satan when he comes against us. We should learn to quote these verses to defeat the attack of the enemy, even as Jesus did when Satan came against Him. Certainly we must recognize the need for this defense.

If it is the offense we need, then we will desire to memorize those verses that deal with God's promises to us to provide for our needs as we make the journey of faith.

In war, and in most sports, the best defense is a good offense. We do need to learn to use the Word of God both defensively and offensively, but I urge you to try to excel in claiming all of the good promises that God has made to His children.

Please read the 28th chapter of Deuteronomy remembering that all God has promised there to His people Israel is also for us today, because we have a better covenant based on better promises. Become skilled in the Word if you expect to receive all that God has promised us through this great key, the Word.

11

A Hindrance to the Keys

Actually the prayer of faith cannot fail. If it could, then the Word of God would not be true. Heaven and earth can pass away, but not God's infallible Word. (Matt. 24:35.)

However, many, many times it does seem to fail. We should be asking ourselves, "Why?"

It seems that a chapter on failure is always fitting in any book written on the subject of faith or prayer. Generally, the most common cause of failure is simple unbelief.

Unbelief is a commonly used word, both in Scripture and in conversation. Biblically, it is not an Old Testament word; it is used only in the New Testament. But Paul uses the word "unbelief" in reference to Israel's being "broken off" in relation to the promises of God, and further warns that we are to fear lest we share the same fate. (Rom. 11:20-22.) To be broken off from the fulfillment of the promises God made to us is fearsome to contemplate.

It happened to God's people Israel. This event is especially sobering when one remembers that Israel saw, witnessed, and experienced more miracles of mighty deliverance than any of the people who lived before or since.

The children of Israel were the people who witnessed a steady stream of God's mighty miracles, signs and wonders. In Egypt they saw the plagues He sent upon the Egyptians: the water turned into blood, the frogs, lice and locusts, the murrain on the cattle, etc. These people experienced the passing of the death angel over them, the mighty Red Sea being rolled back, the water gushing from the rock, the miraculous provision of the manna and quail, the pillar of fire to lead by night and the cloud by day.

But unbelief welled up in their hearts and destroyed what faith they had. Unbelief not only prevented their immediate entrance into the promised land, but eventually cost them their physical lives in the wilderness when many of them died as a result of their sins. We marvel at the unbelief of these Old Testament saints, in the light of so many miracles.

We must not forget that Jesus also marveled at the unbelief of that generation which witnessed His miracles in the New Testament. He not only marveled, but Mark 16:14 tells us that after His resurrection "...he appeared unto the eleven as they sat at meat, and upbraided them with their unbelief and hardness of heart." Rightly did He scold them, for the Scriptures call unbelief *evil*. (Heb. 3:12.) What is evil about unbelief? Why can't we just consider it the negative of faith? Why did the writer of the book of Hebrews go so far as to label it evil?

First, unbelief can rob one of his experience of salvation. Regardless of what thousands of pastors preach and teach, one can lose his salvation if he chooses to do so.

Without getting into all of the theological arguments, we can say simply that when one receives Jesus as Lord and Savior, he is saved and has solved the sin question. However, in receiving Jesus he does not lose his will. He can yet decide to turn back into sin if he chooses, and many do so. This truth is obviously taught by Scripture.

It is never a question of God's faithfulness to keep him, or a question of the veracity of God's Word. It is a question of whether or not a person can make a one-time decision and think that that is all he ever needs to do to be saved.

Unbelief can separate us from the promises of God, and that is what we are talking about in this study. Unbelief is evil in every way. Not only can it rob us of our salvation, but also of any of the promises that God has made to us and our loved ones. Unbelief, while not negating the promises, can hinder their fulfillment.

We see an example of this negative power of unbelief in Mark 6:1-6 which says that Jesus "could...do no mighty work" in His own home town of Nazareth, "because of their unbelief." While He was not stopped completely, He was thwarted from doing the mighty works that He had done in other places. He was so hindered that He laid His hands on only "a few sick folk" (v.5). This was far different from other places where He healed *all* who were sick.

Jesus called unbelieving people, "warped, wayward, rebellious." (Matt. 17:17 AMP.)

One might ask, "How does unbelief fit into the question of the prayer of faith?"

The last report I read shows that there is a higher sickness rate among the clergy than our national average. Does this apparent problem of unbelief begin with the clergy (even pentecostal) and filter on down through to the saints?

Are our people not healed because they do not believe in prayer for the sick? Or is it simply because it is sometimes easier to go to a doctor and take medicine than to believe God for healing? Is there a serious problem among God's people who just simply ignore this part of God's plan of salvation which includes physical healing? Or do we have a very serious problem with unbelief, which is *evil*!

12

The Key of Worship

In John 4:19-26 the Bible records the conversation between Jesus and the woman at the well:

> **The woman saith unto him, Sir, I perceive that thou art a prophet.**
>
> **Our fathers worshipped in this mountain; and ye say, that in Jerusalem is the place where men ought to worship.**
>
> **Jesus saith unto her, Woman, believe me, the hour cometh, when ye shall neither in this mountain, nor yet at Jerusalem, worship the Father.**
>
> **Ye worship ye know not what: we know what we worship: for salvation is of the Jews.**
>
> **But the hour cometh, and now is, when the true worshippers shall worship the Father in spirit and in truth: for the Father seeketh such to worship him.**
>
> **God is a Spirit: and they that worship him must worship him in spirit and in truth.**
>
> **The woman saith unto him, I know that Messias cometh, which is called Christ: when he is come, he will tell us all things.**
>
> **Jesus saith unto her, I that speak unto thee am he.**

The Calvinists believe that all things in heaven and on earth are firmly in the hands of Almighty God and absolutely nothing can, or will, happen unless God originates and controls it. Thus, all of the bad and all of the good must be attributed to God. Because of this teaching, God receives the blame for many things that Satan causes. If Calvinism is true, then even worship must originate with God and be controlled by Him.

The opposite of the Calvinist belief is the Arminian teaching which stresses that God has given man a free will to choose whom he will worship—even Satan—if he so chooses! It is very difficult for me to believe that the only people who can come to God are the ones He has predestined to do so. If God has selected them, then they are obligated to worship Him. He will, then, have only worshippers who are predestined by sovereign choice.

Jesus told the woman at the well, "You worship you know not what." If she was one of the predestined worshippers, how could she "know not what" she was worshipping? This concept would put God in the place of being confused. Here He would have selected someone to be a worshipper, but failed to tell her who she was to worship! But the hour is coming and even now is, Jesus told the woman, when there will be *true* worshippers.

Did a sovereign God fail to produce true worshippers up to this time? Or was worship hindered by the fact that God had given mankind a choice and, through bickering and quarrels, they had split over physical things (such as where they were to worship) and as a result God was not receiving the worship due Him? Is worship a result of God's choice and selection, or is it the exercise of man's free will? If it is God's choice, then how can we know who are His "selected ones" and how can we determine who is worshipping correctly? If it is our choice, then let us begin right now to worship Him in spirit and in truth!

Let us suppose that you attend a church which was preselected for you by your parents, that was preselected for them by their parents, and their parents before them. In such a case, you would have no way of knowing what the worship was like in that church 100 years ago when the original selection was made. Was it a beautiful, free-flowing worship? Or was it about as dead and dry as it is now? Will you continue to attend a church that does not lift up its collective voice in praise and adoration with the lifting of hands as the Bible teaches?

There are several things God's Word commands regarding true worship. Do you know what they are? In 1 Timothy 2:8 Paul writes: "I will therefore that men pray every where, lifting up holy hands, without wrath and doubting." In Psalm 63:4 David writes: "Thus will I bless thee while I live: I will lift up my hands in thy name." Jeremiah exhorts us in Lamentations 3:41: "Let us lift up our heart with our hands unto God in the heavens."

Does it sound, from reading these verses, that we have an option of how to worship? This is of prime importance. Does God's Word teach us that worship is only with the spirit, or does it teach us that worship involves the total tri-nature of man—his spirit, soul and body?

In Romans 12:1 Paul writes:

> **I beseech you therefore, brethren, by the mercies of God, that ye present your bodies a living sacrifice, holy, acceptable unto God, which is your reasonable service.**

The *King James Version* uses the expression ''reasonable service.'' Other translations use ''reasonable worship'' (Conybeare), ''spiritual worship'' (*The Revised Standard Version*), ''spiritual service of worship'' (*The New American Standard Bible*), ''as an act of intelligent worship'' (Phillips), ''reasonable (rational, intelligent) service and spiritual worship'' (*The Amplified Bible*). The Apostle Paul is literally begging us to present our bodies as a part of our worship.

> **For we know that the whole creation groaneth and travaileth in pain together until now.**
>
> **And not only they, but ourselves also, which have the first fruits of the Spirit, even we ourselves groan within ourselves, waiting for the adoption, to wit, the redemption of our body.**
>
> **Romans 8:22,23**

This passage refers to the fact that our spirit and soul are now redeemed, but the redemption of our physical body is still to come.

Most of us know that our body is an enemy of our spiritual growth! When we need to fast, our body puts up a valiant fight. When we desire to spend time in prayer, it immediately gets drowsy. When we desire to read our Bible, it would rather watch TV or get involved in some other entertainment. It just ''goes along for the ride,'' protesting every spiritual step we take!

If we can come to the conclusion that Paul literally meant for us to get our body under control in order to present it to the Lord in our worship, then we can only conclude that every church that does not practice this is in violation of God's Word. It seems that about

90% of traditional churches do not allow for the lifting of the hands and voice in adoration and praise to God in public worship.

These same church members, along with the rest of us, will go to a ballgame and praise the achievements of athletes by shouting, screaming, and clapping their hands. But when they go to church, it is only to "be still and know that He is God." There are many times when we need to be quiet before the Lord, but not always.

Israel was exhorted to praise God with a "loud noise" (Ps. 98:4) and to play upon "high sounding" instruments (Ps. 150:5). Our Father Who, in the Old Testament, loved and received loud praises and joyful music is not suddenly going to reverse Himself and command us to no longer praise Him and sing joyful songs.

When we are believing God for the answer to a specific prayer and we are buffeted by doubt and fear, we can take heart in the great lesson taught in Joshua 6. This mighty leader brought the children of Israel through a great testing time when doubt and fear could have turned to unbelief if they had not learned this powerful lesson. Joshua had the great honor of leading the Israelites into the promised land, an honor Moses missed because he struck the rock in anger.

The walled city of Jericho loomed large before them. A failure here could have caused all foregoing events to have been in vain. Joshua wanted to be sure no mistakes were made. He gave the orders that were to be passed along. The children of Israel were to march around the walls once a day for six days in strict silence.

Not a sound was to be uttered until the seventh day when they were to march around six times in silence, and only on the seventh time were they to say anything—and then they were to shout!

Why, for twelve long, hot, dusty trips around the high-walled city were these people to keep their mouths shut? Why did Joshua command such a thing? It seems Joshua knew something that we need to learn. He knew what kind of comments they would make when they got close enough to see how strong the ramparts were, how impenetrable the massive gates looked, when they realized they had no ladders with which to scale the towering walls! There was no way to stop the thoughts of doubt and fear that would enter their minds because of that which they would see! The insurmountable walls of the city were fact.

What was it that Joshua knew, that we can now learn by reading this account? He knew what thoughts would come into the minds of the people, so he commanded them to keep silence while they marched. **Unbelief in the mind will not get into the heart if it does not pass through the mouth!**

Dear reader, whatever has been your course of action in the past, learn to control your body—especially your tongue! Worship the Lord with all your soul, spirit, and body. Do not waver in your faith. Do not allow unbelief to rise up. If it comes, do not express it orally! Keep on believing. Keep on confessing God's Word, and give His Word a chance to work in you.

> **Now we know that God heareth not sinners: but if any man be a worshipper of God, and doeth his will, him he heareth.**
>
> **John 9:31**

This is a powerful verse that not only teaches worship but also teaches another great principle—the knowledge that when we know that God hears our prayer, then we know that we have the answer. The *King James* translation seems to be the only one that retains the word "worshipper." Most others use the words "God-fearing." The Greek word is *theosebes* and means *"reverent of God,* i.e., *pious" (Strong's Exhaustive Concordance).* Yes, this is a true translation, as you can see. God does hear the worshipper, that is, the one doing His will.

> **And this is the confidence that we have in him, that, if we ask any thing according to his will, he heareth us:**
>
> **And If we know that he hear us, whatsoever we ask, we know that we have the petitions that we desired of him.**
>
> **1 John 5:14,15**

To be God-fearing is not enough. In America our churches are filled every Sunday morning with God-fearing people. But what would happen if someone stepped to the pulpit and asked them to stand, lift their hands and their voices in praise and worship to Almighty God, to be as demonstrative in church on Sunday morning as they had been at the ballgame on Saturday evening! There would be wholesale, vehement refusal! These people would say they were God-fearing, that they had been raised to worship the Lord wholeheartedly—but actually they do not worship God with all their spirit, soul, *and body.*

Notice that Jesus informed the woman at the well that God seeks out those who will worship Him "in spirit and in truth" (John 4:23). This confirms the Old

Testament declaration of Psalms 22:3: "But thou art holy, O thou that inhabitest the praises of Israel." God truly seeks the worshipper. He does come down, as it were, and indwells the place where worship and praise take place. His presence can be felt. True worship must be of the spirit, involving the soul and the body.

It is important that a worship service not be dominated by one or two people. If we allow one believer, in the exuberance of his experience, to worship louder than the others, it will distract and draw away attention from God. We should come before God to worship as a choir, in unison and in harmony. Pastors should so teach this principle that even the visitor will sense how to fit in and flow with the worship. Some pentecostals of the past have not taught along these lines and have allowed some otherwise beautiful times of worship to be disrupted.

I believe there is a difference between praise and worship. Praise is defined as "to commend the worth of; to express approval or admiration," while worship means "extreme devotion, reverence, intense love." We reward with praise people who do things well. God is deserving of praise, for He is constantly doing good things for us. God, alone, should receive worship and adoration, for He alone is perfect and worthy of worship.

Spiritual worship, the kind that involves the total man (spirit, soul, and body) is truly a great key in the Kingdom of heaven. The author has been involved in a portion of the great revival of this twentieth century—a revival that not only has brought many souls to Jesus, but has seen the establishment of great churches. He has seen churches go from a few members to thousands in a matter of a few short years. He has seen many denominational people—both Catholic and Protestant—receive the baptism of the Holy Spirit. He has seen churches that seem to have been frozen into a set form of traditional church service suddenly break out into services in which the worship is beautiful to behold and to participate in! Such churches become part of a new thing that God is doing. It is so easy to become comfortable in traditions. Every time the Spirit of God moves, He has to tear us loose from inherited worship customs that have lost their original meaning.

Today, the Lord is helping us to break out of a mere few seconds of vocal praise into a beautiful, lengthy span of true worship in the Spirit. We pray that God will continue to help us to develop this key, not only in public worship as a congregation, but also when we spend time alone in His presence.

13

The Origin of Sickness

The keys to the prayer of faith will be better exercised if we have a thorough understanding of the origin of sickness.

Dr. T. J. McCrossan in his book, *Bodily Healing and the Atonement*, says that the first verse in our Bible to relate sin and death is Romans 5:12.

Wherefore, as by one man sin entered into the world, and death by sin; and so death passed upon all men, for that all have sinned.

Williams translates the expression "death by sin" as "death as the consequence of sin."

Doctors Van Cleave and Duffield in their work, *Foundations of Pentecostal Theology*, state: "Sickness is in the world because of sin, which is in the spiritual realm, and the activity of Satan, who is a spiritual being. Therefore, its original source is spiritual." (p. 371.)

Death is the result of sin, and sin is the result of Adam and Eve's disobedience to God. Death is the result of disease and sickness. If disease and sickness had not come into the world then there would be no death.

I believe that most all scientists will agree that the human body is so wonderfully and beautifully created that it could live eternally.

The healthy human body renews itself periodically. For instance, we could go barefoot for a lifetime and not wear out our feet. But if our feet were made of steel or the hardest of woods, they would wear out and be gone long before we would! Our bodies are wonderfully made. It takes sickness, virus, or germs to kill the body...if accident doesn't get it first.

Death passed upon the whole human race as a result of sin. When Jesus came to take care of our sins so we would not be eternally lost, He also took care of sickness so we could live longer and fulfill our years here on earth.

Jesus defeated the one who causes sin and death. His name is Satan. One might be quick to ask if that means we will not die a physical death. No, because our mortal, physical body must be changed to an eternal, glorified one. We would not want to live eternally in earthly, human flesh. God has a better body for us—one which can enjoy love and fellowship, food and drink, and yet not be earthbound.

The Bible teaches in 1 Corinthians 15:35-58 that one day we shall be given a new body. I urge you to read this portion of Scripture for a good understanding of death and resurrection. Satan, not God, authored sickness and disease. Viruses and germs are his weapons and under his control.

> **Forasmuch then as the children are partakers of flesh and blood, he also himself likewise took part of the same; that through death he might destroy him that had the power of death, that is, the devil.**
>
> **Hebrews 2:14**

Please notice the last part of this verse, "that had the power of death, that is, the devil." Following are different treatments of this portion of the Scripture by other translations.

> ...that held the dominion of death, That is the Adversary...(Rotherham).

> ...whose power lies in death—that is, the Devil...(*The Twentieth Century New Testament*).

> ...Who had death at his command (*The New English Bible*).

> ...the lord of death, that is, the Devil (Conybeare).

Yes, Satan has the power and dominion of death. It is under his control.

As a young pastor it bothered me to be taught in college that I was to say at the graveside ceremony, "God has *taken* out of this world the soul of the deceased." I changed that to say that God has "received" the soul of the deceased.

Because of a great lack in understanding, even among many pentecostal pastors, many dear saints do not realize that Satan, not God, is the author of death. As a result they are constantly asking, "Why did God take my (child, spouse, parent, friend, etc.)?"

God does not (by death) take anyone. Satan does—usually through sickness or an accident he has perpetrated. Our greatest proof of the doctrine that Satan, not God, is the one who causes sickness and death is found in studying the ministry of our Lord Jesus when He was on earth.

In Luke 13:11-17, Jesus dealt with a spirit of infirmity that had bowed a woman over for 18 years. Jesus blamed Satan for her infirmity, not God His Father. (v. 16.) In Mark 9:25 He referred to the affliction of the deaf and dumb child as a spirit and cast it out. In Acts 10:38 we are told, "How God anointed Jesus of Nazareth with the Holy Ghost and with power: who went about doing good, and healing all that were oppressed of the devil; for God was with him."

I believe that most all Bible scholars will agree that Jesus healed by casting out spirits. Most of us who believe this will not say that *all* sickness and accidents are directly attributable to Satan. Because of sin, viruses, and germs that are in the world, good people as well as evil people are afflicted by disease.

It is also a well-known truth that many sicknesses are due to stress, worry, resentment, and other psychological factors. Many accidents are caused by carelessness, drugs, drinking, etc. In this chapter I only want to deal with the *origin* of sickness and death. They originally came into this world because man obeyed Satan and disobeyed God.

We are indeed in a world controlled by the devil. In the prayer of faith we must take authority over Satan and over sickness. Just as Jesus rebuked sickness and took authority over it, so must we exercise this authority in the prayer of faith.

Please notice in Luke 5:13 that when Jesus touched the leper, the leprosy departed from him. In my opinion, a sickness that departs does so because it has some form of intelligence to do so. This man's leprosy left because it recognized a higher authority—the authority of Jesus! In the prayer of faith, sickness will also recognize a higher authority and leave. (Read carefully the chapter on how to pray the prayer of faith.)

14

The Master Key—
The Name of Jesus

This chapter will not need much amplification by the author. The Word of God is so powerful in its use of that Name above every name. Somehow I feel that we have lost some of the authority of the Name of Jesus. Not so much as it relates to prayer to the Father in His Name, but the simple use of it as a master key when we come against the wiles and the works of the devil.

Let us begin our consideration of the Name of Jesus where Scripture begins, with the announcement to Mary and Joseph.

> **But while he thought on these things, behold, the angel of the Lord appeared unto him in a dream, saying, Joseph, thou son of David, fear not to take unto thee Mary thy wife: for that which is conceived in her is of the Holy Ghost.**
>
> **And she shall bring forth a *son*, and thou shalt call his name *JESUS*: for he shall save his people from their sins.**
>
> **Now all this was done, that it might be fulfilled which was spoken of the Lord by the prophet, saying,**
>
> **Behold, a virgin shall be with child, and shall bring forth a *son*, and they shall call his name *Emmanuel*, which being interpreted is, God with us.**
>
> **Matthew 1:20-23.**

Verse 25 says, "...and he called his name *JESUS*."

Emmanuel means "God with us." Every time we use that Name of *Jesus*, God is with us! Using the Name of *Jesus* does not show partiality of one member of the Trinity over another, it includes the Trinity.

Matthew 12:21 says, "And in *his name* shall the Gentiles trust."

In Matthew 18:5 Jesus said, "And whoso shall receive one such little child in *my name* receiveth me." This verse could easily have been overlooked for the past 2,000 years. Have we literally done this? I do not remember doing so, personally. Perhaps the lesson to learn here is not only the power of Jesus' Name, but also a lesson in humility.

In Matthew 18:20 Jesus said, "For where two or three are gathered together in *my name*, there am *I* in the midst of them." Perhaps when we gather, instead of opening the service rather routinely as we often do with a traditional prayer to which no one pays much attention, we should have a powerful acknowledging of the presence of *Jesus* and what He can do because of *His* presence with us!

If the acknowledging of *His* presence is not strong enough to provoke our imagination so that we can enter into worship with enthusiasm, perhaps we need to pray with more fervency. This also ties in beautifully with His last words, "Lo, *I* am with you alway" (Matt. 28:20).

> **And John answered *him*, saying, "*Master*, we saw one casting out devils in *thy name*...."**
>
> **Mark 9:38**

This is a remarkable verse. It is a direct contradiction of the teaching of so many that only the disciples worked miracles in *Jesus'* Name and that the miracles stopped when they died. But here is a man, not one of their number, and the disciples want to forbid him to cast out devils in *Jesus'* Name.

Jesus said, ''Forbid him not: for there is no man which shall do a miracle in *my name*, that can lightly speak evil of me'' (v. 39). Simply put, the *Name* of Jesus is so powerful that anyone who is not ''against'' *Jesus* can cast out devils in *His* Name. This includes all believers.

> **And these signs shall follow them that believe; In *my name*....**
>
> **Mark 16:17**

''These signs'' include casting out devils, speaking in new tongues, taking up serpents and not being harmed, laying hands on the sick, etc. Proving again that the name of *Jesus* is so powerful that any believer can use it with authority...and ought to do so!

> **If ye shall ask any thing *in my name*, I will do it.**
>
> **John 14:14**

> **Verily, verily, *I* say unto you, Whatsoever ye shall ask the Father in *my name*, he will give it you.**
>
> **John 16:23**

This is double blessing! Whatever you ask *Jesus* to do, *He* will do, and whatever you ask the Father in *His Name*, the Father will do.

> **...and that believing ye might have life *through his name*.**
>
> **John 20:31**

...and be baptized every one of you in the *name of Jesus Christ* for the remission of sins.

Acts 2:38

In the *name of Jesus Christ* of Nazareth, rise up and walk.

Acts 3:6

And *his name* through faith in *his name* hath made this man strong.

Acts 3:16

Just substitute your need and believe for a miracle in *that Name*!

By what power, or by what *name*, have ye done this?

Acts 4:7

...that by *the name of Jesus Christ* of Nazareth...doth this man stand here before you whole.

Acts 4:10

...for there is none *other name* under heaven given among men, whereby we must be saved.

Acts 4:12

...that signs and wonders may be done by *the name of thy holy child Jesus*.

Acts 4:30

...rejoicing that they were counted worthy to suffer shame for *his name*.

Acts 5:41

...a chosen vessel unto me, to *bear my name* before the Gentiles, and kings, and the children of Israel.

Acts 9:15

Anyone who bears the *Name of Jesus* before people surely can be counted as a chosen vessel, as was the Apostle Paul.

...how he had preached boldly at Damascus in the *name of Jesus.*

Acts 9:27

Men that have hazarded their lives for the *name of our Lord Jesus Christ.*

Acts 15:26

But Paul, being grieved, turned and said to the spirit, I command thee in the *name of Jesus Christ* to come out of her. And he came out in the same hour.

Acts 16:18

And fear fell on them all, and the *name of the Lord Jesus* was magnified.

Acts 19:17

...but also to die at Jerusalem for *the name of the Lord Jesus.*

Acts 21:13

There is therefore now no condemnation to them which are in *Christ Jesus.*

Romans 8:1

Unto the church of God, which is at Corinth, to them that are sanctified in *Christ Jesus,* called to be saints, with all that in every place call upon the name of *Jesus Christ our Lord....*

1 Corinthians 1:2

In the name of our Lord Jesus Christ, when ye are gathered together, and my spirit, with the power of our *Lord Jesus Christ,*

> **To deliver such an one unto Satan for the destruc-
> tion of the flesh, that the spirit may be saved in the
> day of the** *Lord Jesus.*

1 Corinthians 5:4,5

These two scriptures are so powerful. They teach us that we have the same authority in the Name of Jesus to commit a Christian, who has with full knowledge openly sinned, over to Satan to be destroyed in his body so that his soul may be saved. This authority is awesome and should only be acted upon with greatest caution. But again it emphasizes the power of the *Name of Jesus.*

Time and space will not permit me to take you to every verse that mentions His Name. We know that we are justified in *His Name,* we give thanks to God in *His Name,* every knee shall bow and every tongue shall confess *that Name,* whatever we do we are to do in the *Name of Jesus,* churches are to assemble in *His Name,* and we are to have *His Name* glorified in us.

We are commanded in the *Name of Jesus* to withdraw from any brother who walks disorderly. There is one mediator between God and man, the man *Christ Jesus.* We are to anoint the sick in *His Name,* and we are commanded to believe on the *Name of Jesus Christ.*

Last, but not least, *His Name* is called the *Word of God.* May we as a Church be more aware of the power and use of the *Name of Jesus.* Sickness, devils, and all opposition to the Gospel must obey *His Name.* Let us use it, that master key, the wonderful precious Name of the Son of God, *Jesus.*

References

American Standard Version. Copyright 1901 by Thomas Nelson & Sons and 1929 by International Council of Religious Education. Published by Thomas Nelson, Nashville, Tennessee.

The Amplified Bible, New Testament. Copyright © 1954, 1958 by The Lockman Foundation, La Habra, California.

Bodily Healing and the Atonement. Dr. T. J. McCrossan. Re-ed. by Dr. Roy Hicks and Dr. Kenneth E. Hagin. Copyright © 1982 by Rhema Bible Church.

The Emphasized New Testament. Joseph Bryant Rotherham. Published by Kregel Publications, Grand Rapids, Michigan.

The Epistles of Paul by W. J. Conybeare. Published by Baker Book House, Grand Rapids, Michigan.

The Modern Language Bible, The New Berkeley Version In Modern English. Copyright © 1945, 1959, 1969 by Zondervan Publishing House, Grand Rapids, Michigan.

The New American Standard Bible. Copyright © 1960, 1962, 1963, 1968, 1971, 1972, 1973, 1975, 1977 by The Lockman Foundation, La Habra, California.

The New English Bible. Copyright © 1961, 1970 by the Delegates of the Oxford University Press and the Syndics of the Cambridge University Press. Published by Collins World, London, England.

The New Testament: An American Translation. Edgar J. Goodspeed. Copyright © 1923, 1948 by the University of Chicago. Published by the University of Chicago Press, Chicago, Illinois.